101 Awesome Things To Do With Your CHILD
& Other Musings Of A Divorced Dad

Dedication

To my son, Noah.

The world is an incredible place filled with wonder and magic. While you look at me and hope to someday be like me, I often look at you and wish I was more like you.

Always be open to the world around you and believe that everyone has something to teach you.

I love you, pup.

Dad

Introduction

I was divorced shortly after my son Noah was born. He was the first kid I had ever really been around and I taught myself how to be a dad along the way. I guess that's what all of us parents do, right?

His mother and I share equal custody of him. I am grateful for the shared responsibility of nurturing and guiding our son. I know I am a lucky man to have this opportunity in my life.

When I first held Noah, I thought to myself, "If I can do this one thing right, if I can honestly say in 18 years I was the best parent I possibly could be, then perhaps all of my mistakes, all of my sins, all of my shortcomings, all of my failures could be forgiven."

So here is a collection of my thoughts, stories and some lessons about parenting that I have learned so far.

I hope you find inspiration and share these awesome activities with a child in your life.

Sincerely,

Robert Urban

Table of Contents

Author's Note

I think it is important to tell you about the structure of this book. This is a collection of thoughts, stories and memories that I have collected over the years that I wanted to weave together, but sometimes there is no common thread. So as you read this list of AWESOME things to do with your child, you will also have some of my own thoughts and writings about various things interspersed along the way. Please note that many times when I wrote, I put the subjective "He" but this was just for readability instead of putting "he or she" every time.

Like most lists, let's start with number 1.

1. DOMO ARIGATO MR. ROBOTO

This is a great rainy day game! Buy a roll of aluminum foil and wrap your child's arm with it- turning him into a cyborg! (That stands for cybernetic organism for those who missed The Terminator.) If he is comfortable with it make the transformation complete and wrap him up completely in foil, effectively turning him into a robot. Ask him to talk like a robot. We like calling friends and family using a robot voice. See if any of them respond talking like a robot. This is also a great opportunity to show your child the dance "The Robot" and when it is cool to dance like that in public- (the answer is never). As they grow older, you may want to consider building a robot together from an inexpensive kit.

2. WHERE ARE MY KEYS? (OR "INCREASE MEMORY RECALL GAME")

A fun activity that engages the mind and increases memory skills is called KIMS. Simply lay several items on a tray (i.e. playing card, a matchbox car, a book, a pen, etc) You give the person 30 seconds to stare at the various items and then take them on a walk, run, do push-ups, swim or some other physical activity. At the end of the physical activity ask them to list and describe the items. This game is a fun way to teach children to pay attention to details.

Rob's Random Facts:

The name is derived from Rudyard Kipling's novel Kim. In that novel the game was used to train and improve Kim's memory.

2

3. WHO WANTS TO BE A MILLIONAIRE?

Noah is only 8 years old, so it'll be a few years before he opens a checking account or pays his first electric bill. But it's still important for him to understand the value of money -- how it's earned, how we spend it and ways to save it.

Once when attempting to get him to shut off the lights when leaving a room, without a lot of real progress, I decided to take a different approach. I showed him the electricity bill every month and explained that some bills are the same every month and some we control. I told him that if we make more effort to not waste energy that is money we don't have to give the company.

Taking this a step further, I told my son that we would try to beat all of the bills we control and that we would split the difference if we beat it. For example our electric bill was around 140. Our next one was 110. I showed him that there was a 30 dollar difference and gave him 15 of that. While it's your decision to give him the difference, I think it is a good incentive.

Perhaps instead you can put the money towards a movie night or something for the entire family to enjoy since everyone was involved in conserving the energy.

Noah and I talk often about the value of money. I tell him that money is only as valuable as the experiences it brings you. Experiences are what create happiness. Money is merely a tool that allows greater experience. The truest treasures in my life couldn't be bought or sold at any cost, but were and are earned instead. Friendships, laughter, love- these are the things of worth, of value.

4. WE CAN'T EAT CORNDOGS FOR BREAKFAST...EVERYDAY

A great way to encourage healthy eating and persuade a picky eater, is to have your child choose one or two meals for the entire family. Remind them that it has to be healthy and fit within the budget you set. Depending on the meal they can even help prepare the food and set the table.

It's never too soon to teach your child about smart shopping. Even at a young age they can benefit from grocery shopping with you. At the store show them how to compare prices, brand names versus generic, how to read labels and decipher what is healthy.

Noah and I play something we call "The Numbers Game." We find an item and see if we can find the same item (size, quantity, etc) for a lower price. Any chore you do with your child can be enjoyable by making a game out of it.

5. BREAK BREAD TOGETHER (UNLESS YOU ARE GLUTEN-FREE)

Learning to cook is a skill your children can use for the rest of their lives. It doesn't have to be some elaborate meal, it could be anything. For things that are more complex, set age appropriate tasks. It's true that including the kids in cooking meals requires time, patience, and some extra clean-up, especially when the children are younger, but it is well worth the effort. Time spent together in the kitchen is fun – and you never know, you might have a little chef in your home!

Did You Know? Eating regular family meals together has been found to discourage obesity and eating disorders.

We are all busy, squeeze in as many moments with your kids as you possibly can. A simple activity such as cooking together allows that.

6. MIND YOUR MANNERS

Take the time to actually teach him to shake someone's hand. Teach him to look someone in the eye when doing this and the appropriate accompaniment. "Nice to meet you "sir" or "ma'am" is a good default greeting when meeting one of your co-workers or adult friend. It may seem a little draconian but I also don't let my son say "yeah" to a grown-up as an answer. It is "Yes" or "Yes, sir". I promise you this level of respect will do wonders for your child as they grow up and this habit is taken into corporate America. If you have a son, teach him to open the door for a lady and to be a gentleman. If you have a daughter, teach her how to be a lady worth a man opening a door for her- not because she can't, but rather, because she is worth it.

Teach them proper phone Etiquette-like not texting in the middle of dinner.

Rob's Confession -I'd be the worst 911 Operator. ''Uh, ma'am I think you mean he is lying in a puddle of his own blood, not laying.

ROB'S TANGENT TIME!

Warning- Possibly Sexist Misogynistic Offensive Rant Following:

I am old fashioned. I believe that a man is the protector, the provider, the defender. He should be strong and tough as nails and kill the bugs and check out the downstairs sounds. He should also be kind, gentle, supportive of his wife's goals and dreams and do his equal share of chores. Yes, I believe a man should cook, clean and be able to do his own damn laundry. Within this role lay the inherit responsibility to ensure the safety, happiness and security of his family.

I am today the harbinger of scorn for men who have forgotten what real men are. I somehow thought that men still took risks. That we still endured hardships with resolve. That we still faced challenges with courage. That we still took the roll of protector/provider seriously. That we were still... Men.

What the hell are we teaching our sons?

I consider myself lucky for knowing many people who are doing a damn fine job of parenting. Many of my friends are great parents and have some damn fine kids that I am proud to know.

Attention: We are not doing our kids favors by coddling them! Let them fail. Let them work hard. Let them sweat. Let them learn the value of and the character that an honest day's work brings.

When Noah grows up, I hope he will know better than to run from responsibility. I hope that the things I teach him now will stick with him as he matures. **Everything good is on the other side of sacrifice and hard work.** I trust that I have taught him through example. We accept our mistakes and are responsible for our choices and actions. He will not think toughness is hiding behind a gun or a gang. He will respect senior citizens not because of who they are or what they did, but rather because of who he is. I remember I held the door open a few years ago for a business woman and she was a little irritated at me and snapped, "Oh, you are holding the door because I am a woman?" "No," I replied, "I am holding the door open because I am a gentleman."

Noah will respect cops, military, teachers and the like not because of the individual actions or sacrifices or even my friendships, but rather the institutions they represent.

He will appreciate the work of the janitor or other "menial" workers because they are working.

He will not live like a parasite off the good-nature of some woman that loves him. He will be every bit the man his father is and much, much more. He will be a real man in every sense of the word because I'll kick his ass if he's anything less.

I regress...I can't speak for women, but I would think they want a real man as well. A man that is tough, willing to die for them and doesn't take longer to get ready than she does. Not machismo, but character driven. A man whose word means something, who can fix stuff and looks someone in the eyes when they shake hands.

Once again, this is not intended to say in any way that men are superior or that the workplace pay disparity or proven glass ceiling of women is right in any way, but just that we are built differently and men should act like men.

7. CLEANLINESS IS NEXT TO ~~GODLINESS~~ SANITY

The definition of what is clean and picked up vary from house to house. Whatever your standard, it is great in teaching responsibility to have your child pick up their own toys. One of the rules we have at our house is that you must first put up one toy, before you get out the next. Obviously the "Let's see how fast you can pick up" only works a few times before that game loses its magic. Some people like having charts and checklists in their houses of daily/weekly checklist. Allowance. I will talk more about allowance later, however I feel that in the beginning it is important to set the expectations that we do chores just as something that comes with part of being in the family. As they grow older and tasks become more difficult, then maybe incorporate an allowance/commission to start teaching financial responsibility.

ROB THE GIVER

To the woman this morning with the three screaming kids in Altamonte Springs Walmart: If you're wondering how the condoms got in your cart....You're welcome.

8. R-E-S-P-E-C-T

Teach him to respect people who work. When appropriate I thank people for working on the weekend when they are helping me in a professional capacity. I always call someone "Sir" or "Ma'am" if they are working and I am not-regardless of age. This teaches him that you value and appreciate the sacrifice of others. This is also a good segue to discuss minimum wage and how much harder laborers work. Discuss your first job and the differences in pay and environment from then to now.

Rob's Parental Warning!! I brought up child labor and the advent of child labor laws in early America. Be warned, that your child may try to use the new knowledge of these laws as a defense against chores.

9. CALL OF THE WILD

In my opinion, the most important factor of being a good parent is spending quality time together. No matter the toys or material possessions they have, it can never compare to simply being with you, their loving parent. It is so much more than merely occupying the same space. Being in the same room while he is watching TV and you are texting your friend about plans for next weekend, is not what I mean. Being attentive, caring and interacting with the child is priceless. These special moments are what shape them as they grow and create meaningful memories for the rest of their lives. They might even teach you a thing or two.

Spending time in nature may not be appealing to everyone, but time outdoors provides endless opportunities for fun with your child. In this tech-heavy age where all of our time seems to be spent indoors staring at a computer screen, nature literally provides a breath of fresh air. When you're outside enjoying nature, you don't have the distractions of the daily grind and life can seem much more peaceful.

When exploring nature, keep in mind there are some safety measures you should take. When hiking through the woods or even in some parts of your backyard, your child should know how to identify and stay away from poison ivy.

Safety Tip. How to Identify Poison Ivy to Keep You & Your Child Safe

Poison ivy is a vine that can grow as a single plant or a bush. If growing near a tree or fence, it will twine around and create a vegetation which cannot be safely crossed. The oils on the leaves of the plant can cause irritation to the skin, itching and blistering. The plant has three leaves. The middle leaf has its own small stem while the two outer leaves connect directly to the vine. The stem is typically dark red in color. A simple rhyme to teach your child about how to identify poison ivy while playing outside is: "Leaves of three, let them be!" or "One, two, three leaves I see , Watch Out, Watch Out, Leaves Don't Touch me!"

God Bless the man who first looked at a beehive and thought- "Those bastards are hiding something delicious in there, I know it.

10. THE BIGGEST AIRPLANE EVER

Make a Paper Airplane out of the largest poster board you can find. Some things you can talk about as you build your airplane are: Pilots, WW2, people that are related to you in the military and what they did, history of flight and the courage of Orville and Wilbur Wright, thrust, lift, aerodynamics.

Perhaps color or paint the plane and tape super heroes to it. Make a competition out of a multitude of designs and see who has the best distance or accuracy or make a target and see who can hit it.

Rob's parenting tip: Use a hot iron for some really sharp creases in your plane

11. AM I TOUGH?

Allow your child to try to crush your hand and comment on how strong he is becoming. Don't wince or make a sound- teach him to be brave and not allow little things to bother him. You will be amazed at how much this will teach him to not whine about minor "boo boos" Your son wants to be seen as tough in your eyes. Teach him that toughness is balanced with compassion. As a matter of fact, if you can watch Old Yeller without crying then you need a heart transplant.

Rob's Thoughts..."Without embracing sorrow, grief, anger, and sadness we limit the full realization of our humanity. Only with every color on the palette can you truly realize what a beautiful and incredible portrait we all are."

12. DON'T BE A HOVER MONSTER

Wouldn't someone twice your size hovering over you be intimidating? Don't hover over your child when disciplining or correcting him. Get down on one knee and rationally discuss what he did wrong. I don't allow Noah to say "I don't know" or to shrug his shoulders at me when I ask him about a poor choice he made. That's a cop out. You may have to prompt him with the true answer if he can't figure out what you mean. For example, "Do you mean to say the truth is I jumped on the couch because I thought it would be fun?" Then let him know that's what you always want to hear- the truth.

Teaching your child early in life to communicate with you no matter what the circumstances and to always take responsibility for his actions makes things easier as he becomes a teenager and young adult. As they get older and understand the world better introduce tact...a way to tell the truth without hurting someone's feelings.

ROB'S TANGENT TIME-

(You Can't Say The Word Beautiful Without Starting It BE YOU)

It's much easier to love yourself when you are being yourself. So be yourself. Be quirky, be silly, be random, be uniquely and incredibly you. Be the real you- some may not like it and that's fine because in your authenticity you will find deep and meaningful friendships and relationships. If you could only realize how much freedom and power there is in being the person you truly are. People that know and who accept and love you-the flawed, broken, real version of you...these friendships are life's greatest reward. Put aside the armor, drop the mask, step out of that societal defined box that you really hate that you live in. Fit in- Why? What to wear, how to look, what is cool, what is normal- screw it all- do you. Shuck the media

11

defined prism of what is beautiful, what is funny, what is cool and define those things for yourself. I got a call at three in the morning a couple days ago from a friend who was hurting. I was so honored he could be real with me and appreciated the depth of our friendship and that he trusted me with his pain. In pain, full of mistakes, poor past choices, too fat, too skinny, ugly, scarred, broken, scared, angry, sad, addicted, mean, liar, cheat, scoundrel, bitch, whore- however you perceive yourself to be, there is SOMETHING incredible about the real you. You are wonderful and awesome. We throw those words around easily but think about them...wonderful is an old Saxon word that came to mean the emotion associated with such a sight, and awesome is something that inspires awe- The real you, the authentic you, the flawed you is wonderful, awesome and capable of amazing things so surround yourself by people that not only allow, but encourage you to be you.

13. BOOK 'EM DANO

Call a fire station or police station and set up a tour. When these brave heroes aren't saving lives they don't mind taking a few minutes out of their day to show a kid around. Take some pictures of your kid in the truck while at the firehouse and tell him what they do. Talk to him about safety procedures and meeting points in case there is a fire at your house.

If the police station has an empty lock-up show him that and teach him about why we have rules and the consequences if we do not obey them.

Note- not the best place to show off your handcuff lockpicking skills- you will get some dirty looks from the cops that aren't your friends.
Me... What Did I do? – The horse that you rode in on

14. IS THIS REAL CHOCOLATE?

"I would rather my son come home with lice, than with a fundraiser"

So some fundraising people aren't going to like this one, but hell the World's Finest Chocolate taste like crap and a majority of those prizes are low budget knock-offs anyway. So world's (not) finest chocolate, wrapping paper, candles, running laps, whatever- Just Say No. Say "no" when your child asks you to call all your friends and family to ask them if they want to pledge money for some school thing. Instead ask him to show you the prize list and pick out what prize he wants most, or think of something. Write down a list of extra chores he could do to earn the money for that and if appropriate you can call your friends and family and ask if they have any extra chores he could do for them. I tell my son I will match the amount he earned and give it to a charity of his choice. This teaches him about the value of earning something he wants and about what charities are, and why in particular people are passionate about certain ones.

"Why did I buy this? I'm never gonna eat this garbage?" *Donates to food drive for homeless and thinks "I'm so nice and such a giving person!" -All of us

15. FLORIDA SNOWBALLS

We live in Orlando, Florida. The likelihood of enough snow for us to have snowball fights are about as high as his mom and me remarrying. Take a spiral notebook each and rip out all of the pages and crumble them up to simulate snowballs. Build a fort out of pillows or take it outside and have a fake snowball fight. When laughing and exhausted teach him that every snowflake is unique and no two are alike. (I still have difficulty believing this). Then explain to him that he is unique and tell him what characteristics are special to him and what makes him awesome.

Another Science Fact- Doing science homework with Noah years ago. Me: "Noah, the universe is filled with protons, electrons and _____?

Noah: "Morons"
Me: "Well, yeah, but the answer they are looking for here is neutrons"

16. XXX-SODA

We don't drink soda in our house. We have X-Soda. Maybe because I am a bachelor I can get away with this, but X-Soda is simply a gallon of water with Xs written all over it. This is the only jug that Noah is allowed to drink from directly. He has a quart and I have a gallon container. (It has Xs all over it so no guest in my house ever accidently drinks from it). Active kids rarely drink enough water and are almost always somewhat dehydrated. Making their own X-Soda allows them a fun, very easy way to drink water. The surprising side benefit is it almost always ensures they will choose water over something else when they are making choices outside of the house.

ROB'S TANGENT TIME!

Why I Am Divorced

Sometimes I wonder why my mind lets my heart be the designated driver. When I married Noah's mom, I was at a time in my life when my idea of courage was that you fight until the death, never give up (one of my tattoos says "Be Brave, Be Daring, Never Give Up") and I foolishly allowed this Marine Corps appropriate thinking to also steer my relationship thinking. I had to be right, I couldn't compromise- no surrender. So inevitably to follow suit- a divorce, the lowest point of my life. Not saying that it was my fault, or hers but rather it was my definition of what love was, what being a man was. In the months to follow I looked at where I had gone wrong, what I had failed, my shortcomings and learned some incredible truths; about myself, about life and love in general. One of the things I realized is that surrendering out of love is a purposeful decision. Not compromising who you are, but rather acknowledging the fact that someone's happiness means more than you being right or having your way. This emotional acquiescence is not a weakness, but rather a noble and virtuous action- one of strength and courage- with happiness and serenity as the reward. Once I recognized that the relationship had served a divine purpose—that the experience had happened for me, not to me—I was able to move on. Last night, when Noah was practicing his homework, I had to tell him to slow down, take his time and write neatly (for those who have seen my chicken-scratch feel free to laugh at my hypocrisy). In the scheme of things it only took him a few more minutes than it would have with him rushing but the final deliverable was so much greater than the initial effort. Aren't things in our grown-up lives just as worthy of a few more minutes of that relaxed attention? So today, take a moment of relaxed attention and define your dream and go after the things you want. We should all embrace new challenges and go on new adventures and change the world for the better. Yet know that seeking sometimes means deliberately searching for something that isn't always meant to be there at the end. This is okay because it is often the journey itself that changes where we want the destination to be...and this is why the heart should drive. Life is not logical. It is not a linear system with flow charts and deterministic effects of those choices, but chaotically beautiful and should be navigated from the heart/soul with the mind as a front seat chaperone.

17. PARENTING POP QUIZ

We often tell our children how to behave, the difference between right and wrong, and make suggestions about how they can improve. Ask them the same thing about you. Ask them if they have any areas they think you need improving on as a **parent**. Ask them if there are things that they think you should work on. Sometimes the answer will surprise you.

Often we tell our kids they need to work on this or that, but a difficult question I learned to ask is "How am I doing as a dad? What things do I need to work on?" This trust and open communication is going to show its strongest return when your child becomes a teenager and really has the tough questions and obstacles. I never want my son to be afraid about talking to me about anything- especially his mistakes, fears, and shortcomings, because that is where our experience in life matters the most.

Remember you're a parent: Sometimes kids need the chance to completely be enveloped by your love and your protection. When my son has a bad dream, I am not going to try to get him to overcome the fear on his own just to teach him a life lesson- I am going to show him that I love him and that everything is okay by wrapping him in my arms and hugging him. They need a safe haven where they can still be a kid and know that mom or dad can be trusted. This also teaches them it's appropriate to ask for help when an obstacle won't budge. Even as adults there are things that we can't or shouldn't do alone. Sometimes it takes strength to ask for help and this is a good way to instill that-however be mindful of the balance of teaching too much dependence on others. Don't let your children confuse being stubborn with being perseverant.

18. AMERICA'S GOT TALENT- HOME EDITION

Find a song you both enjoy. Blare it with the windows down and the
music cranked. Sing along at the top of your lungs.
(Our song is "Eye of the Tiger")

ROB AT THE GROCERY STORE

I went up to a beautiful woman and gave her my phone number in
roman numerals and told her if she was as smart as she was pretty
dinner was on me. I am fairly convinced my next wife will be met at
the grocery store. I will also never be too old to throw random stuff
in people's grocery carts when they aren't looking.

Me: "Noah, Do you want some breakfast?" Noah: "What are my
choices?" Me: "Yes or no."

19. ASTRONAUTS AND FIREMEN

Ask them to write down (or write down for them if still very young)
what they want to be when they grow up and why. You can gain
some valuable insights into what they find important.

Rob's Confession- When I was a kid, I wanted to be a fireman. Now
that I am an adult I want to be a giant super-powered fireman.

20. 1600 PENNSYLVANIA AVENUE

Write a letter to anyone in office and politely ask for an
autographed picture. Include a self- addressed, stamped envelope.
Use this as a lead to explain our political system, other political

systems, and the importance of voting and why you vote the way you do. You can also discuss issues that are important to you. Ask them what they think about issues as well and tell them about a leader you admire.

I am a huge fan of Ronald Reagan so in turn, my son is as well. A running joke in our house is What Would Reagan Do? I asked Noah once if he wanted a veggie burger or regular burger and he responded, "Dad, would Reagan have eaten a veggie burger?"

21. "WHAT'S MY NAME AGAIN?"

Show your child his name in different languages and the meaning of his or her name.

(Rob's Shopping Tip - Many high end flea markets have shelves with prints of these)

You may want to take this a step further and make a family tree. Teach him about his heritage. Tell your child the story of how you came up with his name.

Noah was drawing on a notepad and showed me a bunch of squiggly lines he had made. He said excitedly, "Wow, Dad did you know I can write in Japanese?"

22. TEACH YOUR CHILD ABOUT THE COSMOS

Teach him that we are made of the same chemical elements as the stars. Not just ordinary stars either, but supernovas. Show your child where the North star (Polaris) is. Look at clouds and think of shapes and stories together.

Rob's Science Fact- The best way to find the North Star (Polaris) is to use the aptly named Pointer" stars near the bowl of the Big Dipper, Dubhe and Merak. Just draw a line, between these two stars and extend it 5 times, and you eventually will arrive in the vicinity of Polaris.

23. FORKS- FARTHEST TO CLOSEST TO THE PLATE

Teach your child how to set up a really nice dinner. Extra forks and all. Remind him or her of table manners and how to act in different social situations. Teach them to ask to be excused when finished and if appropriate to ask if help is needed afterward.

Rob's Pet Peeve "Noah, unless you're going to tell me there's a sniper's red laser on me, I can wait for you to finish chewing your food to hear what you have to say."

24. TEACH THEM THEY ARE IN CONTROL OF THEIR PERCEPTIONS

There is no use dwelling on your problems. Pain, someone who wronged you or a life's path that didn't go your way are challenges that everyone faces. We only live for a brief amount of time. (Many tortoises outlive the oldest of us!) When you look back on your life do you want to remember the times you held on to anger, jealousy and sorrow or do you want to laugh, smile, and have fun remembering the good times? We all have crappy days and peaks and valleys, but the great thing about perspective is that it is yours. You control how you want to see the world.

A couple years back some guy in a BMW was speeding and cut me off on I-4. Immediately I thought "Inconsiderate jerk!" Then I forced myself to think that perhaps this was a doctor on the way to save someone's life or he is rushing home for his son's birthday. Improbable, but still possible. I chose to see it that way. It was no longer about me. I felt better about it and was instead now cheering him on and wishing him safe and speedy travels. See the best in others, see the best in yourself, allow for mistakes and forgive easily. Love others, forgive others. Love yourself, forgive yourself.

25. SWEAR WORDS

Real men don't have to use words like "I promise" or "I swear" to mean they are promising something. Your word should be your word. A man should do what he says he is going to do come hell or high water. Your handshake should mean something.

26. TEACH YOUR CHILD ABOUT UNCONDITIONAL LOVE

A few years ago Noah did something trivial and I put him in time out for it. After the punishment was over he came to me and asked me if I still loved him. I gave him a huge hug and reminded him that my love for him was not based on him, his actions or his choices. My love for him had no conditions and was not based on anything he did or failed to do. Outside of our children (and perhaps our pets) I am not sure if I believe in completely unconditional love. However, it is good for us to know that there are people in the world who will give us love and unquestioned loyalty to the limit of their ability. However, I doubt if it is good for us to feel assured of this without the accompanying obligation of having to justify their devotion by our own behavior. Being loved is a responsibility that you should not take lightly.

27. ALL CREATURES GREAT AND SMALL

Noah and I were dog sitting once and in my sleep I accidentally
kicked the dog off of my bed while adjusting my blankets. Next
thing I know the dog is in the corner sadly humming a Sarah
McLachlan song.
Pet's can be like family. They can also teach about the cycle of life
and death (Our Betta fish is appropriately named Sushi #5),
responsibility and so many other things.

ROB'S RANDOM THOUGHTS

I am a people person. I try to be polite to everyone, but there are
times which I enjoy my solitude. I know this sounds weird since it is
not truly solitude but I like lines, yeah likes lines at the bank, The
neatness of this accepted social order gives me the perfect
opportunity to plan my next move, think about the day, etc. I wish I
had transition lenses for when strangers talked to me in public. So
how about (insert local sports team/current weather, topical tv
show) and my glasses would go from sporty nerdy look to
sunglasses telling the offender "don't bother me, you creeper
mccreeperson"

28. CAN THOUGHTS AFFECT WATER?

Through the 1990's, Dr. Masaru Emoto performed a series of
experiments observing the physical effect of words, prayers, music
and environment on the crystalline structure of water. Emoto hired
photographers to take pictures of water after being exposed to the
different variables and subsequently frozen so that they would form
crystalline structures. The results were nothing short of remarkable.
Words that had positive messages had beautiful crystalline

structures and words that were negative had sloppy, ugly structures when seen under the microscope. If this is true and we are made of so much water how does environmental factors play out to your health and your own organic structure? Try this experiment and see what results you get.

29. I HATE POOP MORE THAN YOU.

Toilet training... I hate poop. I mean REALLY hate poop. (Actually I hate snot even more- that nose bulb blower thing made me throw up every time I used it on Noah.)
Luckily I still had a gas mask from my Marine Corps days and I would often wear it when changing Noah's diaper. I have had times where I am in the front yard holding my son up by one leg with a hose in the other spraying him down. I couldn't wait until Noah was potty trained. I am not one of those parents who holds their kids over a toilet for three hours and when they finally go, tell everyone my kid is potty trained. However Noah was trained early.

I did three things to help with this.
1) I threw cheerios in the bowl and told him to sink them. Target practice.

2) I would also tell him there was a microscopic village on fire and only fireman Noah could put it out. (I guess I am to blame if anything ever catches on fire when he is a grown up and he tries to pee on it to get it out).

3) The last is sort of disgusting, but worked for me.
"Noah do you know who hates poop more than dad?"
"Who?"

"The poop monster. He lives in the toilet and poop keeps him away. Crazy that he hates poop and lives in a toilet huh?
So when Noah had to poop he would run to the bathroom and say "Dad, I have to scare away the poop monster"
So I say all the time what works for me may not work for anyone else. Case in point. My brother has an incredible daughter a few years younger than Noah. When they were visiting and she was still potty training, I told her about the poop monster.
My brother called me a few days later to tell me that he now had to go check every time his daughter had to use the restroom to make sure the monster wasn't there. Oops...Sorry about that.

ROBS TIPS ON IMPRESSING A WOMAN

Want to impress a woman? Have a job, be silly, be kind to strangers, be humble, if you are a parent be a good one, open doors and pay for the meal and kill any spiders. Chivalry still works.

30. INDIANA JONESATE YOUR KID

Okay, granted this one takes some work...The payoff is huge. This is one of my favorite memories and worth every bit of time and sweat. Discretely bury a small metal box (or a fancy chest if you are trying to win parent of the year) somewhere in your yard or nearby woods. Create a map with paces from a recognizable landmark. It could be a very simple or very elaborate one-depends on you. (Try the old tea stain trick to give it some age) and sometime later tell your child that it is time for an adventure and make up a story about a map. Maybe put it in a bottle or some other container that would validate the story. Supervise, but let your child follow the map. Tell him or her that if the area has been disturbed and no grass is growing or if it looks freshly raked over, etc that may be the right point and tell them to dig carefully. When they first hear the sound of "CLINK" watch their face. Enjoy whatever treasure you have buried.

31. MONSTERS IN THE CLOSET.

Never tell your children there's nothing there, they imagined it, or there's no such thing as monsters. (Sadly we know there are real monsters out there). That teaches a child that when someone tells them it's not true they quit believing in what they see or believe they see. After all how do we know there wasn't something there? It will also tell them you don't believe in them and don't take their feelings serious. Look where they say, take them out of the room for a glass of water, turn on their light when you are looking. (When Noah went through this once I ran full speed into his closet and tackled his clothes and pretended like there was a small struggle and then came out and wiped my hands and said "Well, they won't be bothering YOU anymore." When you come back tuck them in give them something of yours that protects them until morning. Don't forget when morning comes always give your child a piece of paper to draw the monster or bad dream they had. It helps them connect to their feelings and express it without anyone thinking their silly. Surprise most monsters and dreams when put to paper disappear like magic!

ROB ON THE PHONE

(Or Why More People Don't Call Me)

Actual conversation- "Hey, Rob are you free tonight?" "I am free every night....I am an American. Our freedoms were purchased by the blood of the valiant. Our country was reborn in Guadalcanal, Panama, Iraq, Kosovo, Iwo Jima, Bellau Woods, Afghanistan, Tripoli and countless others. Through the sacrifices of our forefathers to my brothers fighting today, we are all beneficiaries of the democracy, freedom and liberty they've fought to defend. America, with all it's flaws is still my home and I love her. From the redwood forest, to the gulf stream waters this land was made for you and me. "Damn it, Rob. Do you want to come over at 9 for fireworks and a beer or not?" "Sure, see you then"

32. RELIGIOUS STUDIES 101

No matter what your religious or spiritual belief we should always teach our children tolerance in the hopes of a more peaceful world someday. Pick different religions to talk about and study, including ancient ones and spiritual American Indian ones. You may be surprised the thoughts are similar, but the ways of worship may not be. By not being afraid of losing your own beliefs this shows your child to have strength of convictions, tolerance, and to feel they have a right to choose their own doctrine, even if it's not our own. You find more gifts in the understanding of something, instead of the ignorance of it.

33. BLUE FALCONS AND OTHER ENDANGERED BIRDS

Help your children build a bird feeder or find a nice, inexpensive one at your store. This is a great time for them to study the different birds in their areas, and as you find out more and more information about the birds you may learn how helpful they are in the world and what ones need our protection and are on the endangered list.

A REMINDER FROM ROB

A guy was an absolute jerk to me on the phone when I called to talk about a problem I had with something I bought from his store. Instead of getting in a back and forth match with him, I told him - I am sorry if in any way my actions added to your frustration and he broke down and started telling me about his wife and him having problems, his business was hurting really bad, etc and we talked for close to an hour.
At the end he apologized for taking it out on me and thanked me for lending my ear to a stranger (and offered to replace the product).

I was reminded that the meanest, rudest people often need love the most.
Loving others when they don't "deserve" it, is the best thing you can ever do.

34. DO THE FIRST THING FIRST

Teach about task prioritization. Teach about creating lists and sequencing them in order of importance. We have an adage – Do the hard things first. This goes much deeper than just chores. Noah was doing his chores one morning and after emptying the dishwasher asked if he could get some water before moving on to sweeping and swiffering the floors. I said yes and went upstairs to hop in the shower. When I came down he was sitting on my recliner with his feet up, reading the paper with his mug of water. He looked at my face and said, "Water break is over, huh dad?"

"Noah! Why are your clothes in a trail from the stairs all the way up to your room?"
"Dad, the floor is lava and it's the only safe way to get around."
"Pick them up, fold them and put them away."

Next thing I hear is the washing machine starting. "Noah what are you doing, I told you to fold the clothes and put them away." "They had lava on them, Dad."

Noah was packing his school lunch. "Dad, can I have some trail mix?" "Sure champ". I check on him a few minutes later and the rascal had picked out all of the M&Ms from the mix and put those in his Tupperware and left everything else.

Set realistic and concrete expectations of what you define as "done" for any task you assign.

35. PET CARTOONAMANIA

Have your child create a cartoon story about their pets or pet. Even a goldfish or a hamster with a cool name is awesome! This helps them with visualization, creativity, and connecting with their pets or animals in a humorous way!

"I was going home with someone new every night. I didn't even know their names, and you know what? I didn't care." - class hamster memoir.

36. WORD OF THE WEEK

Randomly select a word out of a book or dictionary and use that as the word of the week, trying to naturally incorporate it into conversations and discussions. The Pee- Wee Herman show had something similar when someone said the word of the day, everyone went nuts for a second. (Large Marge still scares me)

ROB AT THE GROCERY STORE PART TWO

We were at the grocery store one night when the person in front of me was talking to the friend he was with. He said, "In Genesis it was Adam and Eve, not Adam and Steve." I don't think they appreciated it when I spoke up and said "actually it was Phil Collins, Tony Banks and Mike Rutherford."

37. BUILD A RUBE GOLDBERG MACHINE

A Rube Goldberg machine is a deliberately over-engineered machine that performs a very simple task. Named after the cartoonist who had a character who would build ingenious contraptions this is actually a huge engineering challenge in many prestigious colleges and awards and money can be won in designing great ones. The internet is filled with easy at home ideas you can easily build.

38. DAREDEVIL

Teach empathy for people who are disabled by having your son or daughter wear a blindfold while at home, earmuffs or not being allowed to talk for only an hour. Guide them around the house. See if they know their house by heart.

ROBS TANGENT TIME

When I Die, I Hope I Can Find Out My Stats

Like how many lives did I change, how many snakes did I walk by in the woods that I didn't see, how many miles did I walk, how many

of the girls that I went to high school with would date grown up
Rob, or other thoughts like... will I ever get to meet my long-time
crush Alanis Morisette or would I have a chance with Famke
Janssen and other wine and jazz induced thoughts.

At the cusp of a new day, before the engine of the world revs up
what do you think about? Do you reflect on how far you've come,
or how far you have to go? Do you focus on your strengths and
successes, or your weaknesses and failures? The best that might
happen, or the worst that might come to be? In your quiet
moments, pay attention to your thoughts. Because maybe, just
maybe, the only thing that needs to shift in order for you to
experience the contentment, love and happiness you deserve is
your way of thinking.

I find that gratefulness changes my perspective and a small ACT of
doing something for someone else with no thought of recompense
will always beat the most grandiose INTENT of doing something.

So today do something small for someone- call them, shoot a text,
remind them they are loved. AND THEN, Do something small for
yourself. Remind yourself that you are worth loving. If you had a
friend that treated and talked to you the way you treat and think
about yourself would you stay friends?

You are incredible and capable of extraordinary things. You are
loved and you are a part of my path. You have the power to affect
and change the world.

39. CHEAP HORSESHOES...USE YOUR OWN SHOES.

Go out into the back yard when it's a nice day. Mark out an area for
shoe toss. Take off your own shoe and throw it at the marks seeing
who can toss the furthest. See how you improve over the spring

and summer. This helps eye hand coordination by trying to hit a mark and increasing your throw. Make it more fun, do it left and right handed. This will improve balance as well.

40. TEACH THEM ABOUT FINANCIAL CHOICES

I gave Noah 30 dollars at the grocery store and told him he was responsible for planning all his meals for the weekend and that I would meet him back in the front of the checkout in 30 minutes. While he was shopping, I bought my food. When we checked out I showed him the receipt for a dinner I took a client out to and then showed him that I had bought all of the ingredients to make the same meal and showed him how much money you can save by making it yourself and the importance of learning how to cook so you can still eat well but at a fraction of the cost and much healthier. As parents our job is to give them the foundation of becoming a well-balanced adult.

ROBS TRIP TO THE GROCERY STORE PART THREE

While in line I got asked by a stranger at the checkout my Final Four prediction-I told him War, Famine, Pestilence and Death. He just looked at me strangely.

41. GET THE DELOREAN

Have your child write a letter to their future selves. Write about their best friend, hobbies, teacher, what they are learning, what they are interested in, favorite food, favorite song, etc.

42. CELEBRATE AN OBSCURE HOLIDAY

Whether it's Talk Like A Pirate Day, National High Five Day or some other "holiday" you can find or make up, have a tradition that you celebrate that is out of the norm.

ROBS NOTE TO ANY OF NOAH'S TEACHERS

Dear Teachers,

Please get to work super early so I can drop Noah off on my way to Panera. I love that place.

Please feed Noah lunch while he's there. Make sure it's healthier than what I offer at home and try to keep it under 2 dollars.

Also, teach him math & science since we rarely practice those in our house and math was never really my strong suit. But, also teach the moral beliefs and manners that I don't teach at home. I want you to reward his successes & know him well along with the 30 others in his class. Please make sure all of your students feel like winners & that no one feels left out and please don't use a red pen because in the "real world" bosses are cool with mistakes. Be on the watch for bullies or trouble makers since I won't ask Noah because I want to think he is tough. (I have been teaching him martial arts and boxing since he was 2 so not really worried about it.)

Don't let anyone mistreat anyone else since I don't have time to find out if Noah is the "different" one. I was sort of a nerdy kid and think he would be better off being labeled as popular. Make sure to recognize each student's individual talents & skills. Tell me what Noah's are during our 10 minute conferences each semester (which is very inconvenient for me- I need to skip Panera to come!!)

Love & cherish my child as if he was your own. I'm busy working 60 hour weeks trying to pay for all of our belongings & don't have the kind of spare time that you do. I deserve making four times what you make because I do important stuff.

Please, also, learn to shoot a gun & bring it to school in order to protect Noah. I highly recommend the shooting accuracy of a Glock 26 with hair-trigger action. It only took me years to become proficient with a gun to where I would feel comfortable protecting someone. Noah is my life & I wouldn't want him to be harmed on your watch.

Please ensure every child that leaves your classroom is safe, smart, well adjusted, & free of social problems or concerns.

As a single dad I occasionally have difficulty parenting my son, but you got a degree in this so you must be able to handle all 31 students with absolute ease. Please don't ever let a bad day or disobedient kid or new policy effect your attitude. I expect a smiling teacher every day. When you're done with this list, let me know. I have more ideas on how you can raise Noah for me.

Thanks, Robert Urban

P.s. I love the folder you paid for out of your own pocket since I forgot to get one although you emailed me the supplies list well in advance , but did you see Noah's new Nikes- completely awesome.

43. HAVE A PERSON OF THE MONTH

Help your child learn about people in other cultures. Good and bad people. People like Ghandi, Mother Teresa, Churchill, Stalin, Mandella, Hitler etc. This can be a great time for children to learn tolerance, ask questions about the people in the world, and try to understand other ways of life.

"MY ARMY WILL KILL YOU ALL! After you try this delicious glazed chicken I've prepared for everyone." --General Tso

44. MUSICAL MOMENTS: OH FOR THE LOVE OF MUSIC!

Pick different music to listen to from the web or cd. Talk about it and get them to understand the different importance of music. Listen to the jitter bug, classical, (pick certain composers) the Beatles, Frank Sinatra, Led Zeppelin, Janis Joplin, Jazz, The Blues, rock N roll, Elvis, The Temptations, Indian music. Spread it out to musicians, types of music, instruments. Include different types of drumming, flutes, and harmonica. The list is almost endless! This teaches them about music's importance in our history and culture. How we grow from culture as a world. Sing with it and lighten up their world! This will show how far back music played a role on a society's social growth.

45. TIME ZONE GAME: FIND OUT ABOUT THE TIME ZONES!

Check out Greenwich Observatory in England a painted line of the international time line. Why it works and what countries are having summer when you are having winter! This helps them understand seasons and time importance by acknowledging the world made up its own time zone! Very cool. Talk about hours and meridian lines. You might even carry it over to a sundial! This helps teach our place in the world and that the world indeed, has its own mind!

ROBS ADVICE ON TOXICITY

Let go of toxic people who dim your shine, deflate your spirit & bring you pointless drama. Politely step away from people who don't believe in you.

Go through your phone and delete every contact who doesn't make you smile when you see their name come up.

Cancel your subscription to their issues; you have enough things to accomplish on the way to your goals without being weighed down by negativity.

I believe that we are all capable of incredible things.

Pursue your dream with a fervor, whatever that dream is.

I believe in you. Now, go chase your stars.

46. EYE CONTACT.

We can be so focused on something and not realize our kid wants our undivided attention. We have a rule at our house that when Noah is talking to me, we make eye contact. Do the same for your kids, put down the phone, pause the game and look into someone's eyes. You can tell when they are hurting but don't say it. You can tell when they are disappointed.

47. TASTE YOUR WORDS BEFORE YOU SPIT THEM OUT

No apology can unsay words. Something said in anger or without truth, was still said and can never be unsaid. Barbs like that scar deeper than any physical injury, especially to a child. I try to think - if this is the last thing he ever heard from me, would I be okay with that? Words are incredibly powerful.

They can cut or they can heal. They can build someone up or tear them down. The wrong words can cause pain, anger, frustration, low self-esteem, emptiness, and emotional withdrawal. (I can still feel the sting of certain words from near 30 years ago.)

Or they can bring enthusiasm, creativity, success, closeness, and joy. They can weave magic and transport people. They can inspire greatness.

On my fridge, on a small magnetic whiteboard has the words "ONLY LOVE" on it as a reminder that only things that emote love and kindness are spoken in our house. One sentence can break a child. Be careful.

ROB'S CHUCK E CHEESE TRIP

After kicking some tail at various games at Mr. Charles E. Cheese we went to redeem our tickets and check out the prizes. Noah wanted a duck dynasty figurine of one of the guys with a long beard. I was surprised that he knew who it was since we don't watch that show. I said you know who that is? "Yeah, Dad....It's the guy from ZZ top"

Parenting PRO TIP – Chuck E Cheese usually opens at 0900. They test most of the machines and leave tickets in them. Get there right when it opens, grab all the tickets, spend 5 bucks and play plenty of games with no crowds, no unruly kids (other people's of course) and leave before it gets crowded.

48. PICTURE THIS

Help your child use and learn about the different art mediums. From pastels, acrylics, oils, water colors, ink, charcoal, to digital. If you can purchase some different ones, its great fun to experiment. You might be surprised by your little Picasso! This is great eye hand coordination and is self-expressive. I believe that there is an artist inside every one of us. Kids have an incredible imagination- let them paint whatever they want. So many free art lessons can be found on youtube and other channels.

Speaking of art...It's sad how Wile E. Coyote is remembered for his violence, and not for his brilliantly realistic paintings of tunnels or clever planning.

49. THE ARTIST EMBRACE:

Take them to art shows and galleries. This is fun and amazing. The art institutes hold so many priceless pieces that it will blow your mind away. Before you go, help them learn about different styles of art, as well as artists and the different art periods in history. This helps them embrace the first creative expression and story telling to create and spread knowledge. Explain how cameras weren't around and to paint it was the only way we have some historical things documented. Ask them what style they like the most or if they have a favorite artist.

50. AND I SAID TO MYSELF- WHAT A WONDERFUL WORLD

Explore The Wonders: Look up the 7 natural wonders and find out what makes them a wonder! Discus your thoughts on it. Check out

the 7 man- made wonders and again your thoughts. Now create
what you think are the 7 natural wonders to you and the man-made
wonders, as well. Show them a few places that you think are
beautiful or inspiring and why you think that. This teaches that the
world is big and beautiful and magical and that man is also capable
of creating incredible things. All the greatest inventors and
architects were once a little child just like them.

NOAH'S RANDOM QUOTES OVER ONE WEEKEND

"Dad, are we going to do any shopping for African-American
Friday?" (Black Friday)

"Dad, these shrunken heads are epic" (He lost dessert for saying
epic- this was a trip to Wonderworks.)

"Dad- the DC universe could totally take the Marvel Universe"

"Noah, how did you cut your arm? "Dad, Being an Urban means not
knowing where 98 percent of your scars come from"

"Dad, you need a girlfriend so you can talk to her about history
instead of me. You should date an archeologist"

51. TELL THEM ABOUT YOUR HEROES

Tell your child about people you admire and why you admire them.
This reinforces teaching your child what your priorities are. Some
of my heroes include Ronald Reagan, Skipper Parker, John Basilone,
Bill Ryland and LaRell Strickland. I wonder if we idolize the people
we do because we like certain traits in them or we like certain traits
because those are what are seen in our heroes?

52. INTRODUCE THEM TO A REAL MAN

A boy needs a father, or father figure, to show him how to be a man. He learns this through example, not just words. He needs to be given swagger, taught how to read life's map so that he can recognize the roads less traveled and the paths to avoid. He needs to be shown what love requires-patience, forgiveness, support. He needs to be taught how to find steel in his heart when life makes demands on him that are greater than he thinks we can endure. He needs an example of the kind of man you want him to grow up to be. Ideally the boy's biological father, but if not around or not a good example a coach or someone at church is often a place to find a good role model. Know that everyone is an example- some of us are good and some of us are bad.

53. PLEASE GET HR ON THE PHONE

Have someone from other cultures answer questions they have about religion, food, traditions and if not intrusive or offensive ask to be included in a custom they share.

Noah once asked a Muslim women in Starbucks if she was a ninja. My plans for that day quickly included cultural awareness training.

"Dad, guess what? There was this navy guy in full uniform at school today so I went up to him and said Semper Fi. He said that's the Marine Corps, I am in the Navy. Noah said, "I know..."

54. TEACH HIM HOW TO DO LAUNDRY AND OTHER HOUSEHOLD CHORES.

"Noah, didn't you wear that shirt yesterday?"
"That's why I am wearing it backwards today, dad."
Sigh...

I am taking the trash out one morning and ask Noah to get a certain shirt for work out of the dryer. I come back and ask him where it is and he says- dad it is dry, but it was really hot and I know you don't like being hot so I put it in the freezer for you. I just hugged and thanked him, made sure it didn't smell like shrimp and put it on.

Noah once fell down the stairs while bringing down his laundry. His first words "Dad, did you see how fast I got down the stairs?" That's my boy!

55. FIND CURRENCY FROM OTHER COUNTRIES.

Noah and I talk often about the value of money. I told him that money is only as valuable as the experiences it brings you. Experiences are what create happiness. Money is merely a tool that allows greater experience. The truest treasures in my life couldn't be bought or sold at any cost, but were rather earned. Friendships, laughter, love- these are the things of worth, of value. I have had the opportunity to travel to many countries and still have currency from them. I show these to Noah and gave him a million lira and talked to him about my trips, about conversion rates, scams and how to fit in to other countries.

ROB' S TANGENT TIME

Depression and Suicide

When I was a child I was the lead in many plays. In one of the plays, I was Scrooge- the embittered old man who had to have ghosts show him the value of Christmas. This past year I was Scrooge- (pre ghosts visit.) and not feeling Christmas at all. My son being out of town for two weeks and having a big empty quiet house to myself does not exactly make me want to ring the Christmas bells and sing Christmas carols. This is called being blue. I am sad and lonely...and I am okay with that because there is a specific cause to my sadness and when Noah returns my sadness will be over. However there are certain people that there is no direct correlation to an event and their melancholy sadness. This is called clinical depression.

One of my closest friends has been battling the demons of depression for years. She is the epitome of beauty-inside and out, but sometimes no matter what, she sometimes just can't shake the blues. She wears a beautiful plastic smile and everyone loves her and she is usually everyone's anchor, but I know the truth- she lives in that place where the razors edge of despair cuts her constantly. A general malaise of the soul. To people like this we say "Just cheer up" like they didn't think of that. Holy Doogie Howser- By Jove I will just be happy- yay!!! Except it doesn't happen like that.

I am one of the strongest willed people you will ever meet. I have an absolutely incredibly high tolerance for pain, cold, discomfort and pride myself on my endurance. Years ago I had to go under the knife and I tried everything I could to fight being put under by the anesthesiologist, but was out in seconds. You see because the human body is a mish-mosh of chemical reactions no amount of willpower can overcome how you are built.

So regardless of the desire to be happy some people just can't be. First of all, let's not kid ourselves, there's still a stigma in this society about having a "mental illness." and since it is unseen it is not as apparent as a cut or broken bone. Having depression is seen as a weakness, a character logical defect, something to be ashamed of. And it is not.

I would put my friend's soul, her effort, her dedication to the betterment of man and her overall character against almost all others-myself included- and comparatively, we would fall short. And although she has rose colored actions she sees the world through a gray hue. And this burden is heavy.

And while I walk beside her in her fight and she has a legion of other people that believe in her, in truth any burden is almost yours alone to carry. Killing oneself is, anyway, a misnomer. People don't kill themselves. They are simply defeated by the long, hard struggle to stay alive. When somebody dies after a long struggle with a disease, people are apt to say, (with a hint of approval), "He fought so bravely." And they are inclined to think, about a suicide, that no fight was involved, that somebody simply gave up. They couldn't be more wrong. For the most part suicide is not the Romeo and Juliet impulse we see on TV's. Suicide is a cold, dark and hard road where you are always trying to get back on course, but never seem to find your way and over the years despite your best resolve, you just want to stop walking on that painful dark road.

My best friend committed suicide several years ago and redefined what I thought about suicide. He was the best man at my wedding and the toughest dude I ever knew- he was Rambo and taught me everything I know about combat. I knew he wasn't a coward....I knew he loved his family dearly...not a day went by that he didn't tell me about his wife and daughters and it was only when he committed suicide that I realized the full extent of mental health issues-the demons that he fought were so strong.

That sometimes the only path you think you have out, the only way you no longer involve your family in the fight is to choose the ultimate way out. Before you end up in the whirling dark despair of uncontrollable medication and white padded walls and become a concoction of three parts tragedy and two parts pills; before you commit actions and words that can't be undone or unsaid you still have control- you still have your dignity, you still have a choice. And you choose to go out on your terms.

And I beg you, don't think this is Rob's carte blanche dismissal that if you chose to end your life that would be fine. Ho hum- Cest La Morte.

Nothing could be further from the truth. It would not be fine. It would break my heart...but I would understand. For those who throw darts of derision I don't think you (or I) could understand the toil and burden that would cause someone to consider this ultimate act.

In my darkest hours- suffering from guilt, sadness, heartache, shame I have never contemplated suicide. I have never thought the battle could not be won or that tomorrow wouldn't be a better day so I have a difficult time writing about this, but I think it is important. Forgive any temerity in me assuming what feeling like that would be like.

There are religions that believe that suicide is a one way ticket to hell. If suicide is a sin so is a lustful thought. So if I have a lustful thought and get hit by a car I am dying in the act of committing a sin. Sin is sin. Sin is missing the mark. It is for another post my beliefs about God and such, but I akin God and his love to being a dad.

There is nothing Noah could ever do that would cause me not to love him, not to desire a relationship with him, not to forgive him, not to want him in my loving embrace and god's love is a thousand fold over the capability I have.

I believe the triumvirate of the godhead knows the toils of your soul and understands suffering through his son's life and will forgive you and love you if it is your desire for him to do so and you will still go to heaven. When I was ten I found a dog that had been hit by a car on the side of the road. I knew that there was absolutely nothing I could do to save him so I put him out of his misery. That was the toughest thing I had to do in my life up until that point. How much harder do you think it would be for someone to end their own misery...They really have to be in pain to be able to make that decision.

So for those fighting the good fight, wearing the fake plastic smile, walking the edge of the line, hold on...Your life means something dear to me and you are loved more than you know. While I can't stop the rain from falling, I don't mind standing in it next to you until it does.

And try to be nice to everyone, because a person looking you dead in the eye & smiling could be hiding a world of pain. "Sometimes even to live is an act of courage." - Seneca

56. WHOSE LINE IS IT ANYWAY?

Sit with your child or children, or children and extra adults. This could be a great party game as well as just one on one. Start a story about anything, get to an exciting part, like, "just when the dinosaur drank the purple water he started to freak out when. . . Let the next person take over, then keep it going. This teaches completion, working together as a team, and listening skills along with creative imagination! And it's a blast!

57. EVEN MORE IMPROV? YES, PLEASE

Another fun game is to take turns telling a story or singing a song where every other word is your responsibility. For example I would start time with "One" and Noah would say "year" then back to me and so on. You will crack up at the direction that the sentences and songs take.

58. TEACH THEM TO APOLOGIZE SINCERELY

Show them to never mess up an apology by trying to include an excuse.

As a general rule when I ask Noah anything (usually more discipline related) he is not allowed to say "I don't know" or to shrug his shoulders as an answer. He interrupted during a conversation a friend and I were having over breakfast. I asked Noah why he did that and he said that he was being selfish and not thinking of the other person's feelings. He then proceeded to apologize to her. To teach someone sincerity, you must first teach them they are the ones responsible.

"I'm sorry." Two simple words and yet two we have a hard time saying it correctly. We easily utter them in response to trivial matters like accidentally bumping into a stranger or when you change your order at a restaurant. Yet in important matters and to those who mean the most to us, we can find ourselves practically choking on the words and not saying it when we should. We expect them to be there tomorrow and often take their presence and forgiveness for granted. Why is admitting that we are sorry and apologizing so difficult? Ego. Apologizing can be particularly hard for men because it involves the admittance of fault. It's hard to say that we messed up. That we were wrong. Our ego gets in the way. Anger. Things that need apologizing for are rarely a one way street.

We probably did something wrong, but the other person probably did too. And sometimes our anger over how they offended us is so great that we justify what we did and can't get past it to apologize. The older I get, the more I realize there are always two sides to every story. So how do we overcome our ego and our anger? Humility. By becoming humble. The reason we put up these walls is that we have an overinflated view of our true selves. We're always right; we always have it together... Yet, we aren't. We're human. We make mistakes. You have to accept your imperfection as a part of life. My best friends know my weaknesses and love me in spite of them. Embracing the fact that we aren't perfect and that we can become better than we are so important in being a man. Don't live your life as though every day you're pleading your case before an imaginary court, presenting evidence for why you are not at fault and are innocent of the charges. . You don't have to apologize for what truly wasn't your fault, but you can find the things, no matter how small, that you could have handled better. I think I was a good husband, however in taking the time to reflect on my marriage and my divorce I knew I had a lot of things that had I known then what I know now, I would have handled differently. (This is why often second marriages are so much better than the first ones in case any single ladies want a free dinner.) Once you apologize for those things that will get the ball rolling for the other person to own up to their mistakes. Don't let pride stop you from being the bigger person and taking the initiative. Apologize soon after making the mistake. The longer you wait, the more resentment is going to build up on both sides, the harder it will be to make the first move, and the more awkward the situation will become. Be a man and nip it in the bud. Often it's much easier than we think it will be. Don't give your fear strength. I had a recent event where I fucked up. I lost sleep over it for days and finally called my friend and apologized. He said "No big deal, man" and asked if I had seen the game earlier. No big deal?! This kept me up for days. Often we make mountains out of molehills. There are times that you shouldn't apologize. Like: For your beliefs. If you offend someone by standing up for your beliefs because you failed to debate like a gentleman and ended up being snarky, attacking the person personally, or generally acting like an ass, then you should apologize for your boorish behavior. However, if you've made a completely respectful argument in favor of your position and a person is simply offended because of the nature of your beliefs, then you should never apologize for that. Don't be sorry for what you hold near and dear to your heart. I am not sorry for anything I say and if you are offended by my beliefs that is your problem, not mine. I speak them with love and respect and intelligence. A constant sorry without effort is just vacuous words and means nothing to me. Take complete responsibility. Never, ever make any excuses while you're apologizing. They instantly ruin the weight and sincerity of your confession. Don't use any "buts." As in "I'm really sorry that happened, but...." A man takes full responsibility for his mistakes. Express your understanding of why you were wrong and the weight of your mistake. A person wants to know that you fully understand the seriousness of the situation that you have thought through exactly why what you did was wrong and the full consequences of your actions. Nobody wants to hear an apology from someone who clearly doesn't know why they're in the wrong but feels like apologizing is what they're "supposed" to do. Prove your contrition with your actions. In the end, words will matter very little if your actions don't match them. After you've apologized, stop dwelling on it. Simply start acting in a way that demonstrates the sincerity of your apology. Move on. Once you've given your sincere apology, don't apologize again. If you continue to grovel then you'll always be in the inferior position instead of having the person treat you like an equal. Either the person accepts your apology or they don't. If they do, then there's no need to keep groveling. If they don't, then the person doesn't trust you and the relationship has other problems that need to be fixed.

To understand being sorry, you also have to understand forgiveness.

If we want to become truly incredible, we have to forgive people when they make mistakes. The most important person to forgive is yourself. You are not your past; you are not your past habits, you are not your bad choices, you are not your failed marriage, you are not who/what others defined you as years ago. You are only who you think you are right now in this moment. You are only what you do right now in this moment. Regardless of how filthy your past has been, your future is still spotless. Don't start your day with the broken pieces of yesterday. Teach your children to forgive themselves and others.

ROB'S TANGENT TIME

Should You Spank Your Kids?

Do whatever you think is right for your household, however here is why I don't believe that spanking is the right answer.

Ask most of the people who know me well in my role as a parent and they will tell you that I am strict. These same people will also tell you that Noah and I have a very close relationship and that Noah is a very polite kid and full throttle.

I worked very hard on building a foundation of trust between Noah and I. I always wanted him to feel that no matter what he could come to me and talk to me-about mistakes, fears, failures, poor choices as well as all of the good stuff. I always wanted him to think I have his best interests at heart and believe spanking can greatly cause your child to question this premise and shake this foundation you worked so hard to make.

Scientifically, some amazing things happen to your body when you think you are about to get hurt. The fear response causes adrenaline and cortisol to flood our brains. Functional priority shifts from the higher order frontal lobe (the cognitive learning center) over to the brain stem (-the instinct mechanism.) It is almost impossible for children to learn something in a state of fear or pain (some things I have read also contribute ADD and other mental health issues to prolonged periods of high levels of cortisol) If you are really trying to make the event a learning scenario (which all punishments to children should be) then spanking takes away from that.

So what's the alternative? Especially with physically tough kids, spankings are ineffective-the amount of pain that you actually have to cause to inflict pain on a kid like Noah would borderline on the abuse side. I believe that everyone has something they love. Take that away. Let the punishment fit the crime and don't make idle threats or unrealistic promises. I have never swayed from any punishment- never made idle threats to Noah about him going to timeout if he does something or something he enjoys getting taken away (dessert for a week).

Communicate in a way that actually teaches, rather than punishes. Don't give chance after chance. Either change your rules or boundaries of what is acceptable or stick with first time obedience. I never tell Noah to do something twice and I have never made idle threats.

"This is the last time I am going to tell you" is the death knell of respect... Don't say it.

The Latin root of discipline means "to teach," while the Latin root of punishment means, "to inflict pain." Know the difference.

To be clear I have spanked Noah. Probably five times in his life and in situations where the danger was so egregious I wanted him to learn just how important it was. (Once for example when he ran into the street after I told him to stay in a certain spot)

I got spanked all growing up and I turned out okay. If you insist on spanking your kids, this is how I believe you should do it.

Do not spank when angry!!! This is an emotional response and almost never handled the right way. Wait until you are calm and talk to the child. Don't hover over them - kneel on their level eye to eye Tell them why they are getting spanked and ask if they have any points of view or details that you may not be aware of. Carry through and afterwards always hug them and remind them that you love them.

I think sometimes with the lectures I give Noah or the talks we have about character and choices, Noah would rather be given a spanking.

59. TRY DIFFERENT FOODS.

We have a rule in our house. You don't have to finish something but you have to at least try it. You never know if you don't like it if you do not at least try. When in the grocery store go down the ethnic foods aisle and dare each other to try something.

One day Noah and I will probably go to a sushi restaurant and be mature enough to resist doing Chopstick Walrus, but that day is not today.

60. ASK DEEP QUESTIONS ABOUT LIFE

Talk, ask about big grand things- ask deep philosophical questions. You would be amazed at the brilliance of children and rediscover your youth- their imagination can be you fountain of youth. Teach them the beauty and importance of communication.

You are made of the same material as stars...Supernovas at that...and you are incredible and capable of extraordinary things.

61. MAKE YOUR OWN TRADITIONS

Make your own routines and traditions that your child may pass along to their children or at least remember with fondness. Here are a few of the routines at our house.

We have family movie night. (pronounced faaaaaaaamily movie night) We alternate who gets to pick the movie each week. Once every couple weeks we will have what we call MST night. (based on the old Mystery Science Theater show)
We pick a movie and we talk over the entire movie-adding our own lines.

We cook together every Thursday night and always have dinner together at the dinner table. All phones and technology is off while we eat.

Family game night-In a world filled with technology and apps, there is something to be said for the old school board games. (We like cranium and chess and scrabble)

Funny accent day. I am horrible at impressions, magic and accents but that doesn't stop me from trying. Noah asked me once in the worst cockney accent if I wanted a spot of tea. I died laughing. No idea where he learned that.

Whenever I tuck Noah in I ask him to tell me the best part of his day, three things he is grateful for, three things about himself that is good, one thing or situation he could work on and then tell him the same for me. This teaches kids self-esteem and reminds them that they are incredible, however we all have room for improvement.

What kind of home environment are you creating? One that you would have given anything to have or one you would give anything to get away from?

One of the Best Traditions I ever thought of is actually something I want to turn into a kids story. The Christmas Gorilla.

When Noah was about 4 I had just put him to bed. A few minutes later I hear "Dad, dad!!" and run up the stairs.
"What's wrong champ?"
"I am not going to be here for Christmas"
" I know that, but we will celebrate when you get back"
"Yeah, but what about all the presents I told Santa I wanted?"
"Well the Christmas Gorilla will take care of those"
"Who is the Christmas Gorilla?"
"Well the Christmas Gorilla only goes to houses of kids who's parents don't live together and gives them presents"
"How does he know what you want"
"You have to write the name of the presents you want on a banana and leave it outside."

So we did that.
When he got back from being with his mom and stayed with me, I played a monkey sound real loud on the mp3 player and Noah comes running down the stairs
"The Christmas Gorilla Was Here!!!"

So we went outside and all of his presents were outside and there was a banana peel left near them. So when he got back to school he told friends that he had Santa and The Christmas Gorilla come and some of them said no such thing. He said of course not for you, your parents are still together. He only visits special kids with divorced parents.

He believed in the Christmas Gorilla longer than he believed in Santa...

GRATEFULNESS IS THE FOUNDATION OF CHARACTER

62. GIVE CAREER ADVICE

To my great surprise I am frequently contacted by friends asking me life advice. (You do realize I have no more of this thing called life figured out than any of the rest of us, right?) Many times they ask me to talk to their kids about the business world. These kids are often finishing up college or high school. They ask ole "Uncle Rob" about what direction they should take in their life, professionally and why. This is, honestly, a seriously complicated question, mostly because I'm usually concerned that the question itself might be the wrong one to be asking. What I want to say, more often than not, is before you think about what you want to do, you have to think of the implications of whatever steps you take. The right question is who do you want to be?

I got an email from a friend of mine the other day who has known me since I was a kid and wrote something along the lines of "I wanted to tell you, I think you are a great dad, I would never have thought you would turn out to be after knowing you in high school (Hard to believe for those who met me later in life that I was an immature class clown, huh?) I told her that the Marine Corps profoundly changed me and the way I viewed the world and I am eternally grateful it did so. It's not hard to imagine that someone who works in a homeless shelter will view the world differently than say someone who works in a clothing store.

I write all that to just admonish you to

"Be careful what job you take, because your job WILL change you."

Because at 35 or 45 we KNOW that the person at 17 making important life decisions doesn't really have the experience to make the choices that we think is best, so we will tell them how to live and the "right path to take." There is a tremendous amount of support for these traditional decisions, and very little support for making any deviating choices. Social constructs and schools side with the interpretation of the right path to take. What school should you attend, what should you major in, what should you do afterwards? People ask me why I joined the Corps. I can tell you mom, dad, apple pie, etc which is partly true, but the real truth, the absolute truth? I had no idea what I wanted to do with my life. I was afraid to be like my dad, who got stuck in a career he hated weighed down with responsibilities and never really following his dream- he was always looking out the window wondering if there was more to life.

So back to the decision. It's possible that the direction we're facing is more a reflection of those structures than it is a reflection of ourselves. Self-determination in a moment like that can't simply be about making a choice, it has to start with transforming the conditions that constitute our choices. It requires challenging the "self" in "self-determination" by stepping as far outside of those supporting structures as possible, for as long as possible.

This is the necessarily scary thing we call the unknown. We don't want to make the wrong choice and because of that we often make the safe choice, not necessarily the choice we believe will make us happy. (This happens in relationships and other aspects of life, not just a career.) I know that the most significant and meaningful periods of my life have all been moments that I could have never rationally chosen or even known as possibilities had I not been foolish or lucky enough to step into the unknown. Any genuine process of discovery is terrifying.

I don't push Noah into being a grown-up and acting older than he is because I have realized that he will be eventually be that. There's no rush to get started early on something that you will always be thereafter. Everything before a career has defined beginnings and endings. Elementary school, middle school, junior high, high school, college. There's always been a predefined end, and that contributes a lot to making the indignities of those institutions bearable.

Once you start working full time, though, it's just One Long Semester that you're expected to attend for the rest of your life. So consider caution if you're overly excited to start down that road as quickly as you can. Other than being forever, it's not as different from what's come before as you might imagine. This is all just to explain why, when kids ask me for career advice, I'm likely to respond with something like "if I were you, I'd do something that you would hardly ever be able to do again. Go sail around the world, go hike the Appalachian Trail, travel to somewhere you always wanted to go and stay there for a few weeks. Go tour with your band My career advice usually falls within the framework of doing the absolute minimum amount of work necessary to prevent starvation, and then doing something that's not about money, completely outside of supporting structures, and not simply a matter of "consuming experience" with the remaining available time. Do whatever — but make it count and that it is your dream.

It would seem like I want a perfect life for you- to have always woken up under the most brilliant rainbow and never have any challenges, heartbreaks or disappointments, but it's your struggle that made you so strong and so beautiful. I wouldn't take that away from you if I could.

63. STOP READING THIS FOR A MINUTE

Go hug and kiss or text your loved ones and tell them that they are special and that you love them.

I remember being a kid in the ocean wishing I was strong enough to slow down the encroaching water towards my sandcastle. As a father I wish I could do the same and somehow slow down time and not see my son grow up so fast. I feel as if I blinked and he was seven. I am so glad that he and I make/have made so many memories to someday look back upon to remember the full measure of these days.

64. THE BEST DATE YOU EVER HAD

Talk to your child about the best date you ever had and what made it great, You can also explain what dating is, what you are looking for in a person to date (or when you dated) and ask them for date ideas- might be amazed at their creativity. Tell them that even if married, you still take your spouse on dates and that romance and love and consideration should never get old.

ROB AT THE GROCERY STORE PART FOUR

It's had been raining cats and dogs all day. I went to the grocery store and a person in his mid 20's was sitting on the ground. You could tell he was waiting for a ride or something. I took my time shopping and when I headed outside he was putting plastic bags on his feet and his work uniform in a separate bag.

I asked him if he needed a ride. He politely said, its about 25 miles away. I responded "I didn't ask where you were going, I asked if you needed help getting there." He graciously accepted and we hopped in my car and talked about the weather and life.

He saw a picture of Noah and we talked about family. I found out he had two kids of his own and a girlfriend. He said that sometimes that he takes a taxi but that's half his day's pay and he works three jobs. I was humbled and silently grateful to have a job that I enjoy, working with creative and brilliant people and just in general for the things I have. In the end it's just stuff, but it's still worth being grateful for.

I asked him what his plans were for the evening and he said he was going to make some mac and cheese for the kids and just head to bed since he had to be at his other job in a few hours. With his permission, I pulled into a KFC and got him a huge family meal and said this one is on me. He still politely offered me gas money when I dropped him off and he thanked me profusely. I told him I was the one who was grateful to meet him.

65. HOW I MET YOUR MOTHER

Talk about how you met their mom or dad and what you felt. Even if like me you are divorced, the child is still half of the other person and telling them that the other person had a great characteristic or you enjoyed certain things about that person makes the child feel self-worth and value.

If Single
It's ironic how emptiness in the heart can be so heavy. We think of past loves and broken dreams more often than sometimes and when we stay in those broken dreams we forget that we are beautiful and life is precious. Make peace with your past and see the beauty in the obvious. Stop feeding yesterday and instead feed

tomorrow. Push on, go the distance and map the uncharted lands of your soul's desire. Answer your calling.

Rob's Dating Advice for Grown-ups- If your girlfriend is mad at you put a cape on her and say, "Now you're super mad!" If she laughs, marry her.

Rob's serious advice for dating- When the love is gone, have the courage to walk away in peace before the emptiness fills with hate.

66. PASS THE POPCORN

Go to a public place, people watch, and make up imaginary stories about people. Make elaborate back stories.

ROB'S TRIP TO STARBUCKS

Noah had been under the weather for about a week so on the way home when he said that he needed to stop somewhere I didn't push the issue. We ended up at Starbucks to use the restroom. When he came out, he spoke loud enough so most everyone in the café hear him say "Dad, this place has the softest toilet paper I have ever used! You have to try it." Thanks son, scratching off that Starbucks makes #434 on the list of places I will never go again.

67. REASSEMBLE, STEPHANIE!

Next time you replace a small appliance, (except a microwave) give the old model to your kid. Together, you can dissect the machine and examine its parts. Don't know much about circuitry? There are little kits that you can buy and you can build radios, lights, even robots.

ROB'S TANGENT TIME

Learn What My New Year's Resolution Is. Every Year.

The promise of a fresh start is alluring to us all. No matter what we did yesterday, tomorrow holds possibility for redemption; we can finally become the "best version of us" that has been somehow held down. We haven't been awesome enough or accomplished enough or kept on track enough, but now's our chance– because it's a New Year!

I find myself thinking "This time I'll really commit to (insert goal here). This time I'll do it!"

Usually, I hold myself to unreasonable expectations or strive to check off too many changes at once. So when I fail to work out one day or don't do some charitable thing for another person I feel like a failure. If I just put in a movie and order a pizza for Noah because it's just been one hell of a day, I feel like I am the world's worst parent.

...But I can do anything.

That's what runs through my head at the start of these clean slates: I'll just MAKE MYSELF do it! I am a badass former Marine with incredible willpower, discipline and resolve.

So then what happens when my best effort that day isn't that amazing, earth-shattering awesomeness that I promised myself it would be? I beat myself up.

We forget about the effort and only see the results.

I slip into the mode of thinking I'm not good enough, that I must change who I am and what I do. It's a self-defeating pattern because striving for perfection is harmful, not helpful. I forget about all the wonderful things I already am and already do, and concentrate on what I'm "lacking" and how I somehow failed to make that bridge to where I am supposed to be.

So, what's Mr. Inspiration do when he realizes that every second of our entire lives are a clean slate? I seize the day.

Life is NOW. I am NOW. This is my moment.

Each time we conquer a self-limiting belief or take a step outside our comfort zone, we've celebrated a fresh start! (Everything good is on the other side of comfort)

By tuning into the moment-to-moment of our own life, we find chances for new beginnings in EVERY decision we make.

I am already enough. Life is not measured in external validation. The most amazing gift we can give to ourselves is the realization that our life and our contribution is uniquely our own. No one could be you.

Sure, I could be healthier, eat more vegetables, be more kind, love more, do more good-there is always room to shine brighter or develop healthier habits or reach more people, but at our core-We are enough.

You are enough...Just as you are.

Holding to that belief and enjoying this moment is infinitely more fulfilling than checking off boxes and lists from arbitrary slates.

So what's my New Year's Resolution?

Being more Me.
That is all.
And that is everything.

68. NFL COMBINE TIME

Build an obstacle course in the backyard. How many pushups? How many jumping jacks? Maybe make it an annual event and turn it into a picnic where they try to beat last year scores or have team versus team of different branches of your family.

69. HAVE A BACKYARD CARNIVAL

Set up homemade stations – darts into balloons, water guns knock over paper cups, have a guess how many pieces of candy are in something, old bracelet around the house use as ring toss, the sky is the limit. Have the games give out tickets that they can redeem for small dollar store stuff. Hot dogs, cotton candy, and popcorn are inexpensive and perfect carnival food.

ROB'S TANGENT TIME

Are You There, God? It's Me, Robert. (My Thoughts On Does God Exist?)

Life's ultimate question. Your belief of the answer and the interpretation of that answer defines your morality and ultimately your life.

I have struggled with this answer my entire life.
Here is a confession.

I have never felt god in a building. I grew up in a Christian home, and faithfully attended what I would consider a good church. Good pastor, people I liked, preached directly from the bible and the music minister, LaRell is someone to this day that I respect more than just about anyone in the world. I remember being ashamed that I never felt the holy spirit move me during church, never felt like God was tugging at my soul, never felt like the lord talked to me...I felt foolish raising my hands during singing or even praying- Was I going through motions, symbols, traditions and rituals that the church had done for centuries.

Was it me? Why couldn't I just have faith like everyone else. Was Jesus knocking on my heart and I just couldn't hear it?

I was once asked what is the one question that, if it was answered, would make you happy, content and at peace with God? I don't have an answer.

I've looked far and wide for what I believe truth to be. You might be amazed at the depth of my knowledge regarding most religions (and science) trying to define what I believe.

I was once told- well right or wrong, what's the disadvantage in believing? Nothing, other than that is not belief, that's hedging your bets.

I was once told- you will burn in hell if you don't have Jesus- Sorry, I am not believing in something just to avoid something.
I buried my friends who were noble and good and thought there is no god.

I saw the Grand Canyon and thought- there has to be a god.

I have seen nature's aftermath in Katrina, Hugo, the Philippines and thought there is no god.

I have held my son for the first time and seen the miracle of life and thought- there has to be a god.

I have experienced my wife miscarrying...and thought there is no god.

I have such a hard time when people use the bible as the source of proof in God. Many of the stories in it are exact renditions of stories, myths and prophecies told in Greco-Roman, Egyptian and Judeo-Apocalyptic societies that predate Christianity by thousands of years (the virgin birth, man being saved from pandemic flood and many others)

But this is logical thinking. This is an analytical scientific dissection. I go back to Noah.

No abstraction, no book, no description, no thought can accurately contain or convey the miraculousness of holding him for the first time. Yet my mind's arrogance insists its thoughts can. So my mind starts spinning sticky, unsatisfying webs of logic, reason, and thoughts attempting to capture to "know" with certainty.

Laws of entropy, law of irreducible complexity (while some systems and organs can be explained by evolution, some biological systems appear to be too complex to have arisen by natural selection) give me rational logical proof of an intelligent design.

So based on logic, I find there is enough proof to not yet accept a Judeo Christian god of the bible, but I can accede to intelligent designer.

So how about morality? Can a person be a good person without this definition of God? I believe in some of the teachings of Christianity, Buddhism and even the cosmic universe connection, but most of all, I believe in me. I don't begrudge anyone's beliefs and sometimes even envy your faith that a supernatural deity will take care of your problems. I wish I could easily accept that- my life would be much easier.

Morality is a cultural concept with a basis in evolutionary psychology and game theory. Species whose members were predisposed to cooperate were more likely to survive and pass on their genes. Reciprocity, altruism and other so-called 'moral' characteristics are evident in many species.

Religious texts are simply part of many early attempts to codify moral precepts. Religion has always been a control mechanism. Secular law, flexible with the shifting moral zeitgeist, has long since superseded religion as a source of moral directives for the majority of developed societies. Secular ethics offers a number of competing moral frameworks which do not derive from a purported supernatural source.

So is there a God?

Believe whatever you want, however whatever decision you end with treat people with love, dignity and respect.

70. TEACH THEM ABOUT WEAPON SAFETY

Even if you are ardently against guns, I still think that teaching them about the safe handling of a weapon is very important. Even just knowing and learning the rules, without ever even touching one can save lives.

The four safety rules are:
1) Treat Every Weapon as if it were loaded
2) Never point a weapon at anything you don't intend to shot
3) Keep your finger straight and off the trigger until you are ready to fire
4) Keep your weapon on safe until ready to fire

71. TEACH YOUR CHILD TO SKIP A ROCK.

To me, there is not much more Sylvan bliss possible than seeing a still lake in the early morning. I enjoy fishing and the tranquility. A dying skill is the ability to skip a stone across water. Here is how to skip one.

- Select a rock. It should be mostly flat, about 1 -2 inches and thin. Triangles and rectangles work better than circles.

- Grip the stone. Hold it with your thumb and middle finger, then firmly hook your index finger along the edge.

- Throw the stone. Snap your wrist at the end your throw and aim for it to be parallel to the water.

DR. ROB'S PROGNOSIS

So I realized this year that I am dying. I haven't told anyone. When I found out, I promised myself that I would be more kind, love more, be a better father, try new things, let petty things slide.

Guess what. You are dying too. We all are one more day closer to the inevitable. So now that you know that you are dying as well is there anything that you would want to change about yourself?

Then why wait?

We are, if anything, creatures of habit drawn to the safety and comfort of the familiar. However a real and fulfilling life can only begin when we step out of our comfort zone and embrace the possibility of failure or rejection and take risks.

We often refer to the human race as a contest and focus on who is winning and who is falling behind. But perhaps the race is not about winning, but more importantly who shows up to run it, and the type of race they run. Many times, the victor is the person who makes the race their own.

The story of me has a happily ever after. I know this because no matter what life throws at me, I'm still the author. You are the author of yours as well.

So tomorrow when you wake up in the morning take a moment to reflect on what a privilege it is to be alive - to breathe easily, to ponder life's questions, to enjoy doing something or to spend time with people that love you. Make the race your own.

72. FOCUS ON GOOD EXAMPLES OF AUTHORITY

Our culture has lost respect for authority mostly because our kids hear the parents constantly complaining about the teachers, government, politicians, cops and other figures. I try to keep my bitching to a minimum around Noah and instead let him hear me say good things about police officers I respect, friends I admire, teachers and coaches I had that were awesome, and politicians or companies that are doing things right. If we don't respect authorities that are in our lives, then how can we expect our children to? I am not saying being automatons with no free speech, but focus more on the good. For every bad cop story I could tell you of a hundred good cop stories. For every 99 horrible politicians out there I can think of one who might be okay. (The people who should be running the country are too busy working and raising kids.)

73. BUY THEM A MUSICAL INSTRUMENT

You can find a very cheap instrument on craigslist, asking friends what's in their attic or sneaking into the high school band room after dark*. (* not recommended)

With most instruments you can easily learn how to play 5-7 chords-that's really all you need to know play most songs. You don't have to have your child master it or make it their life's work to reap the rewards.
Playing a musical instrument benefits you in almost innumerable ways. For one, it'll make you smarter. Yeah, you heard me. Learning to play a musical instrument is tough, and it's been proven to actually increase your memory's capacity as well as your ability to concentrate. And it's not just a temporary thing either; studies suggest that it has a lasting effect, long after the instrument is back in the case.
It's also great for developing your motor skills, it's literally good for your ears, and it can improve your cognitive abilities. It's also been shown to improve your math skills, even if you never learn to read music.

74. TEACH THEM HOW TO SAFELY START A CAMPFIRE.

Not many things can beat the memories of s'mores cooked over the campfire and hot dogs straight from the flames to the plate.

The fires of life burn everyone. Whether it's our own stupid choices, external events, or just random bad luck-at some point in our life we get burned. There are only one of two ways to respond to that. We either whither and crumble and we learn blame, jealousy and hatred or we become tempered like iron and become as hard as steel and we learn forgiveness, gratefulness and appreciation. While we can't control circumstances we do control how we react, and that reaction becomes how you are defined.

75. SET THE EXAMPLE FOR YOUR KIDS TO DREAM BIG

Once at 4 o'clock in the morning Noah came down to where I was working and asked me to make him some bacon. He said, "Bacon for breakfast like a man, huh Dad?" He ate two pieces and some oatmeal then fell asleep on the couch. Sons especially want to know if they have what it takes. They want to see approval from their dad and often for better or worse, emulate the characteristics that the father displays. I tell Noah that our background and circumstances may influence who we are, but we are responsible for who we become. I tell Noah that life is tough, a roller coaster of ups and downs and that my job is to teach him to enjoy the highs while being strong enough to endure the lows. We love our kids and want them to have great lives, easier and better than we had it. What we forget is that overcoming something difficult is what gives us character and true strength in the first place and we are doing them a disservice by making things too easy for them. We want our children to go after their dreams, but do we?

Have you done anything lately worth remembering? What are you waiting for? Life should be a courageous journey or nothing at all. If something feels like it is missing, how do you expect to find it by continuing to do exactly what you've always been doing. Choose to listen to your inner voice, not the jumbled opinions of everyone else. It's your road, and yours alone. Others may walk it with you, perhaps only for a little while, but it's your road. Great days can bring joy, crappy days give you experience, and the worst days sometimes give you the best lessons.

Use these lessons to define who you are. Even the best days have sunsets and even our worst moments pass.

I believe that our instincts are rarely wrong- there is something that just feels right when going along with the current that your heart knows is the true direction. We swim against this current because society, even our friends tells us it's not the right way to go. You have the only compass to your soul. Be who you were born to be – If you want your child to pursue his or her dreams, then you must follow your heart, and be who you are as well. Age and time are just excuses. You can do anything. Regardless of what you decide to do in your lifetime, feel it in every fiber of your bei-ng. Don't waste your life fulfilling someone else's dreams and desires. Be uniquely, incredibly, awesomely you. Define yourself. Make your own life and write the story of you that you hope it to be.

ROB AT 11 AT NIGHT, UPSTAIRS

Noah came up to me one night around nine and asked if I could make him something to eat. I made him a sandwich and said, "I want you to go to bed as soon as that is finished." I was downstairs getting caught up on some work, when suddenly I heard noises coming from his room upstairs. By now it was 11 o'clock. I went to his room and he was playing with his action figures and Legos. "NOAH! What are you still doing up?" "Dad, I haven't finished my sandwich yet" and he shows me an uneaten corner as proof....I was laughing too hard to be upset.

76. TEACH YOUR CHILD YOUR DEFINITION OF GOOD.

Certainly some of us will point to the concept of "character" and "kindness" as key attributes of goodness in any form. Manners are indicative of these traits, but can also be exclusive of a "good heart." (I know some real jerks that say their please & thank yous). I do believe that self-deception makes appraisal of our own goodness challenging. Depending on our psyche we see ourselves better or worse than we are, almost never as is, because we justify things. So how am I to know how honest I am being with myself or, more difficult still, how honest you are with yourself?

From any litmus we are all very imperfect. We all screw up—some bigger and worse than others. We mess up in relationships-no one is perfect at work, with their spouse or girlfriend (boyfriend) nor as a parent and sure as hell not at all three. I could forever list the mistakes I made as a husband, at work, with Noah or as a friend. Here's the seeming contradiction: the more we talk about how we have made mistakes, even very profound mistakes, the more we are free to act and do things that feel good. When we share that gut-wrenching truth about ourselves, it changes not just the teller but the listener too. The definition of goodness, in my opinion, is to be better at everything than you were yesterday; living a life of self-improvement. Our experiences define our lives and every day is a new starting point in this journey.

Ever feel stupid- some mistake you made, for dating someone or some other trivial thing? When you feel that you just did something stupid remind yourself that sometimes sloths grab their own arms thinking that they're tree branches and fall to their deaths.

ROB'S TANGENT TIME

A Must Read For People Going Through Life's Trials...

When I got divorced I felt like I had failed for the first time in my life. Not just at something trivial, but perhaps the most important choice that someone can do. I was crushed that I had to start over- I felt that I was a great husband- loyal, funny, kind, romantic and felt ashamed that someone couldn't love me.

At anything else in life, when I came against an obstacle I just worked harder and would eventually overcome. No matter the effort I put in, there was just no saving the relationship.
We put on happy faces over Christmas because we didn't want to ruin anyone's holidays and would laugh and smile even while we had the court stuff going on in the background. That was eight years ago... Since I had a son and felt committed to take care of my obligations, I was tied in to a state (Florida) that I didn't know almost anyone, all of my family were hundreds of miles away and I felt all of my life's hard work and sacrifice up until that point in my life were moot.

Without any experience dealing with kids, here I was thrust into being a single dad and I made a decision that this kid was going to have an incredible life- regardless of his parent's divorce. This kid was going to be loved and a priority and likewise my life was going to be great. I would use my experience and very diverse set of skills to teach him amazing things. In retrospect getting divorced was the best thing that could have happened. I could parent exactly as I wanted to- the ideas, the boundaries, the discipline, the things I wanted to instill and teach- I didn't have to dance on eggshells or compromise what I believed I should be done in order to keep my wife happy.

My career choices were up to me- what was I interested in, what sounded like fun or met my current priorities at that time- I did it and I never took the safe route. If I got some wild ass idea and wanted to invest money and more importantly time (my very very late nights and early mornings) into ideas and businesses I did, without having someone hold the reins and ask me to pursue safer ventures or more traditional paths.

I have made incredible friends in Orlando and entire families that love Noah and welcome us into their homes and lives and I am so grateful for them and their roles in being the family that Noah doesn't have here. Which brings me to Noah. He is a respectful, kind, adventurous kid with a big heart and a great work ethic and imagination. He (good or bad) has inherited my sense of humor and is a good kid. The times I spent traveling the world and meeting great people weren't for naught, they were things and experiences and people I could share the magic of with Noah and about just how awesome the world and some of its inhabitants were. I could tell him funny or heroic stories about my Marine brothers and exploits and adventures in far off lands with exotic foods and wonders most people will never see.

The whole purpose of me writing this is that for those who are going through a separation or divorce or just struggling by being thrown around by life's winds of change know that it is only the end of a chapter, not the end of your life and that you still have incredible years ahead of you if you choose for them to be. In the immortal words that my Aunt Cheryl (RIP) told me when I told her I was getting divorced. "No matter what, you just weren't her cup of tea...but that doesn't mean you aren't an awesome cup of tea"

77. GET TO KNOW YOUR CHILD'S FRIENDS AND THEIR PARENTS.

One of the best ways that you can positively influence your child's friendships is to stay involved. By getting to know your child's friends, you can gain some insight into the relationships that your child is involved in—and keep an eye on those relationships to make sure that you are okay with them.

- **Create an Inviting Home**- Make your home a place where your children's friends like to hang out. (Healthy Snacks and drinks in the fridge always help!) Get to know them while they are relaxed and open to conversation. Make sure the kids have permission to be at your home and what rules are accepted. For example is their child allowed to play the same video games as yours?

- **Know Their Names**- Learn the names of all of your child's friends.

- **Know Their Parents**- Get to know the parents of your children's friends. You will often find that they share your values and priorities and that you can work together to ensure that the friendships are positive for everyone.

- **Attend School Events** - Whenever possible, attend school events and chaperone on field trips. Ask your child to introduce you to her friends. Spend a few moments asking her friends about their likes and dislikes. Show that you're interested in getting to know them. I love that Noah's school allow me to visit him for lunch and sit with his friends. (Let's see if Noah still thinks I am cool enough when he hits high school.) If doing something local, consider inviting your child's friend.

Noah's field trip consent form lists walkmans & radios under "Optional items."   Where the hell are they going, 1985?

78. MAKE A HOMEMADE PIZZA TOGETHER

What kid doesn't like pizza? Especially when you get to control how much of what goes where. Let them pick what ingredients they want. My favorite homemade pizza are actually made on English muffins, a little alfredo sauce and cheese.

My son wants pizza, but doesn't eat the crust. Then he asks for breadsticks. I just give him the crust back.
Noah tells me that he is really struggling with fractions, especially improper ones. I try to explain them to him by describing a whole pizza and how it is made up of slices. He asked that we get pizzas and cut them into slices so he really understands. I picked up two pizzas tonight to show him and after the second problem he seems to understand fractions perfectly. Not sure if it was that great of an example or if I got conned into getting him pizza.

79. AND FOR DESSERT!!

Make Dessert Sushi.

From either homemade or store bought rice krispie treats, cut portions into small square pieces. Place a swedish fish on top. Use thin strips of fruit roll-ups to wrap around the rice and fish.

OR

Dirt Pudding Cups With Gummy Worms
The first order of business is making the dirt. Place some Oreo cookies in a large zip-top plastic bag and crush them into small pieces. Next, make the pudding. Pour the pudding into a cup, then the Oreos then put in three gummy worms. I made it in Terra Cota pots before but I think that was a little overkill.

Noah and I were wrestling and ground fighting one morning on the hardwood floor. I told him afterward, why don't you buy us a wrestling mat that we can drag out so you don't get hurt. Noah said, "Dad, it's okay- skinned knees and bruises are just a part of life. Happens to everyone."

80. TEACH YOUR CHILD THE DIFFERENCE BETWEEN COST AND VALUE

When Noah asks for something I think is unreasonable, I don't lie and tell him we can't afford it. Rather I tell him the truth. It's not worth it. And I tell him why.

There is a huge benefit in teaching your child about the difference between price and value and asking them to tell you about the value of something they want or their intentions with it if you were to buy it.

For those who know me well, you know I am not a keep up with the Jones kind of person. I would rather spend my money on some rare antique book or nautical helmet because the value that I get in looking at those things at home are worth more to me than the newest gadget or doodad. I will always see the value of something experiential that Noah and I can do together- visit a place, teach him a skill, learn something interesting together and just discover how awesome the world is- a million times more than anything tangible I can own or have. Your children often emulate your priorities. What are you teaching them to value?

I have always believed that in order to experience the finer things in life you must first have to experience the things that they are finer than. I believe we learn from every person and every experience in our life and whether a person has a cameo or revolving role in our life he or she leaves an imprint on the definition of you.

Don't feel as if your child has to have the newest, shiniest toy or that you have to keep up with societal pressure. Have them Save Up and work for things they really want and don't be afraid to say no. We have three rules of shopping for anything he wants to buy.
"No toys that make sound"
"No toys we already own" (I know call me crazy...)
"It has to be in the budget. No Exceptions."

81. TEACH THEM TO BE TRUE TO THEMSELVES

Kids are going to go through stages where they dress and act like their friends. Tell them they don't have to dress or act or talk like anyone else- they are an individual. They have to be real to themselves.
Used wisely, experience is valuable because we can recognize patterns and respond appropriately. It is interesting to note that those few who have learned to be true to themselves and their innermost convictions shine like bright lights in a dim world of deception and pretensions. Give me the flawed version of you because that is real. That is my lighthouse.

What if people knew the real you. Would they like you more or less than they do now? If people could see you the way you see yourself- if they could live in your shoes and have your memories and experiences that formed your character-Would anyone love you? Would they forgive you? - Before we judge others, remember we only see what others allow us to see. Teach your children this:

The brave facade, the plastic smile, the easy laugh could be hiding a dark and terrible scar and a world of hurt.

82. Teach Them How To Be Graceful In a Loss.

While I care so much more about Noah's manners, kindness and character I still grunt and point and say "That's my boy" when Noah excels in some sport. It's not about bragging rights (okay, maybe a little) or in any way that Noah is superior to someone else other than at that time at that specific event, but rather that sports are important because the lessons they teach transcend the (pool, mat, gridiron, field, ring, track, whatever). The human body is the only machine in the world that the harder you work it the stronger, faster, tougher it gets. Laws of atrophy- Everything else breaks down... Theoretically, there are peaks and maxes to a person's physical capacity but I am not sure I agree with that. I believe you can always dig deeper. We can always be better, in every way, than we were yesterday. In this act of learning to dig deep, we learn who we are and exactly what we are made of. Gold medals and first places are great because they validate the return of hard work, however we should also reward effort. I never tell Noah that I expect him to win- I tell him I expect him to give his best effort and have fun and the results are what they are. However rewarding effort is not the same as telling him that he won. We should be fair and tell our children when they lost. That despite their best effort, they didn't win. To do any less is an insult to their intelligence and devalues the times they win. I tell Noah often it is that in life there are bound to be failures, but present in those moments of loss, disappointment and frustration, is the truth. The truth about yourself about how the world sees them and how much weight to give the opinions of others. There are probably only four or five people in the world whose opinion really matter to me. How many people's opinion matter to you? Should they? Take away struggle, disappointment, and heartache completely from childhood and you are left with what will become an incomplete adult. Kid's don't see the long term and it's not easy for parents to teach how today's dark clouds will be tomorrow's successful garden....but it is so important to try to do so. Good parenting is hard work. It's supposed to be challenging, because the job is designed to produce a complex masterpiece. If you don't put time, energy and effort into it now, don't be surprised at the end result when they don't turn out to be the man or woman they could have been.

ROB'S TANGENT TIME

Life...

People fascinate me. No, not the run of the mill square punch in, punch out go to work, go to home people but more so the broken, the daring, the scarred, the risk-takers.
The lessons and stories you learn from those who risked, the resolve you learn from people that went through what you would imagine is an impossible ordeal-yet here they stand, can teach you so much.

I was speaking to an old friend of mine the other night whose mom passed away last year-the hardest blow in a series of unfortunate events during the past year and we talked of success. "Sometimes success is not winning or being on the mountaintop, sometimes it is just being able to tie a knot and hold on while life throws her worst at you"

I have an incredible network-friends from all over the world, people from every walk of life- homeless beggars that know my name and call me friend to nobility I have dined with and everything in between. Give me the weak, the cracked, the flawed among us because they are the strong, they are the beautiful. And the truth is.... we are all flawed. We are all so ashamed of our imperfections against the public mirror that we fail to realize that we are our biggest critics. But you shouldn't be... Although you should "know yourself and seek self-improvement", you should also be your own biggest fan.

Not braggadocio or peacocking, but rather- wow I have the ability to be incredible. I can make a difference. I matter. Because you can and you do. I'm smart enough (and realistic enough) to know that life is not perfect. Mine is no exception. Life is often hard-fought, and often the happy moments are long sought-after and we worry when the next great moment is going to be. Perhaps the reason we are so worried about this "great moment" and all the moments that cram themselves into that short time is our collective inability to see the good without looking for the lurking, ever present "not-so-good." I struggle with that.

My life is the stuff of dreams and I have to force myself to not think, "When will the other shoe drop? These long-awaited perfect moments sneak up on you. The ferocity with which they make their entrance leaves one stunned. When something this big happens, we expect to see it coming for miles and miles, however the truth is, the greatest moments in life find a way to lie in wait for the right time. They listen when we do not. They follow us, echoing our hopes. They fill our soul and our heart. They become the beat that we follow as we dance through life. Before we know it, we are right in the middle of the greatest moment we can imagine. The great moments do not come by accident. We do not stumble upon them by happenstance. You must learn to listen for the gentle knock of great opportunities. You can't do that in a web of negativity. Life sucks for all of us every now and then...Divorce, friends' death, failures-I have been at the valleys. I have walked at rock bottom. If you are there, then I challenge you to find courage. The root of the word courage is cor—the Latin word for heart. Courage originally meant "To speak one's mind by telling all one's heart." Over time, this definition has actually changed, and today, courage is synonymous with a Marine being heroic or someone performing brave deeds. Heroics and bravery are important because they remind of us of the potential of the best of us, but I think we've lost touch with the idea that speaking honestly and openly about who we are and about our experiences (good and bad) is the ultimate act of courage.

Heroics is often about putting your life on the line. The courage that brings happiness is about putting your vulnerability on the line. In today's world, that's pretty extraordinary. I don't believe that you can love yourself or others without being honest...vulnerable, allowing your shield to drop and letting someone into your castle walls. The people I love deeply know my weaknesses and still choose to call me theirs. And that is a beautiful thing. "No one can change the past, but we can determine what is next" Know that you are loved. Believe in yourself. I am rooting for you.

"We hate what we do not understand." I'm not exactly sure what that phrase means, but it's stupid!

83. ENCOURAGE HAND- WRITTEN LETTERS

In a day and age where communication is as simple as point and click, there is something to be said about the thoughtfulness of a handwritten letter.

Noah was making a homemade Mother's Day card for his mom with the nicest handwriting I had ever seen him do. I asked why he doesn't write like that all the time and he said that he saves it for special occasions.

84. VISIT A CHILDRENS CANCER WARD OR BURN UNIT.

Your life will never be the same. Have your child play with other kids and teach your child empathy and compassion (and selfishly gratefulness). When we were registering Noah for school we passed a kid in a wheelchair and Noah gave him a high five. I asked if Noah was friends with him and Noah replied "I am now". We should all have the hearts of children.

In the rare occasion I get sick and Noah hears me throwing up I pretend I am a mother bird feeding her kids or a pterodactyl. It helps me think about something else other than not feeling well and lets him know I will be fine.

85. TEACH YOUR CHILD THAT WE ARE ALL CONNECTED. THAT WE ALL MATTER

I believe that we are all connected. That each action, each person, each act is purposefully woven together into the fabric of the cosmos. Intuition, gut feelings, random thoughts are the universe's prompting us and nudging us to a certain course of action. From a scientific perspective (Fibonacci Sequence, fractals and chaos theory mathematics, etc) the universe is anything but random. The ripples of our actions echo throughout time and space. Your smallest kindness matter. A smile, a simple hello, a word of encouragement... Even if I am wrong about the universe being effected by it, a person's world can definitely be and sometimes that matters just as much.

It is a dark, lonely, bone chilling existence to find oneself, but also the only path to a meaningful life.

86. TEACH YOUR CHILD TO ACCEPT RESPONSIBILITY FOR THEIR ACTIONS

A pair of dirty sneakers lay in the middle of the living room floor. "Noah, why are these shoes in the middle of the floor? That's not where they go." "I didn't put them there" "So a thief walked into our house, decided to not steal any of the things we have and instead just took a pair of shoes and put them in the middle of the floor?" "Maybe... perhaps he was trying to send you a message?" "Noah, put your shoes up on the shoe rack." "Yes, sir.

The "Someone else is to blame," is as old as the creation of the world-Adam and Eve. They ate of the forbidden fruit and instead of taking responsibility for their actions, they started to blame others. Adam blamed Eve and Eve blamed the serpent. (I wonder if one of them had said, "God, it is my responsibility" if they still would have been evicted from their Utopic garden?)

Instead of admitting that we are wrong, mean, impatient and inconsiderate, selfish and egotistical, we try to place the blame on someone else. Maybe this is because we don't want to be perceived as weak or a failure-and by accepting responsibility we have to look at the mirror and accept we fall short of perfection. We are all flawed in some way and what's ironic is accepting these weaknesses is actually a sign of strength. Blaming others is a poor character trait. Not simply because everyone can see through it. Or because it's dishonest. Or because it destroys relationships. Or even because, while trying to preserve our self-esteem, it actually weakens it. There's a more essential reason why blame is a bad idea: Blame prevents learning. Blame prevents growth.

When we attribute our success to our personal characteristics and effort and blame outside variables or others for our failures we lose the opportunity to become better than we are today. I am not saying that other people's actions don't influence us. Our parents have made choices that have helped to determine who we are.

Friends, teachers, employers, the government—all have/(have had) an influence on our lives, and can give us excuses to blame our circumstances on other people. No matter how we got here, our circumstances are what they are, and that is what we need to focus upon. One of the basic tenements of leadership is to accept responsibility for your actions. You want to find a good leader (manager, etc), look for someone who does the following. When things are great or successful he or she points to the team behind them and when things fall short of the mark, they point to themselves.

GREAT LEADERS CREATE OTHER LEADERS, NOT MORE FOLLOWERS

ROBS TANGENT TIME

Broken Dreams

I took some time off recently because I was pursuing a dream. It was something personal and not work related and last night the possibility of that dream ended completely and permanently. I won't go into details about what it was because it detracts from this message I want to write.

One of my closest friends said something incredibly profound to me the other day. I had mentioned chasing something and he asked what it was and I said "my past". He replied "Just remember the past is a place of reference, not a residence."

Dreams are something sacred. There is a magic and beauty to what we can envision for ourselves. No matter how great or extravagant our dreams may be, we all deserve to have those dreams. Not just the important dreams of when we are kids about the future, but dreams that we have today, tomorrow and years from now. Sometimes though, life goes astray from what we had planned and dreams fail. And often the worth we have for ourselves can dwindle and die right beside our dreams because somehow the dream itself became the definition of us. Our worth is not tied into or defined by the success of our dreams. Sometimes our dreams do not come to pass, regardless of the desire or effort for them to do so.

Discussing your goal or dream can make you feel raw and vulnerable and foolish when the people you told of the dream see it not come true. Maybe your soul floods with anger, jealousy, and self-hate over the loss of the possibility of your dream becoming broken-a brokenness that has the power to halt any further dreaming and sense of self-worth. In no way am I saying that broken dreams don't hurt.

When my dream failed last night part of me died.

That's okay because there are a lot of big parts to me. The human heart is vast and capable of having many dreams, many loves. We have to be okay with the outcomes of any choice, acknowledging our worth, move forward, and choose to believe in our future.

Do not be quick to give up on yourself. Sometimes the hardest moments we encounter are ones that will lead to greater strengths and a greater self-awareness. If you are struggling, keep pushing forward! If you have put up a grand fight for your dreams and are realizing they just might not be meant to be, have hope. While the very thing you thought you wanted is not coming to be, your strength and character are gearing up for the best fight yet to come; the road to your newest and deserving dream. After a broken dream it can be easy to limit your abilities, expectations, and wants. Just because something did not work out and you may feel leery of dreaming big again, that does not mean you need to limit or downsize your new dreams. You are incredible beyond measure and capable of awesome things. So buck up, dust off, stand tall and try again.

Happiness is not a place you go to, happiness is not a person, happiness is not a dream you achieve, happiness just is. Happiness is a choice. I choose to be happy. I choose to be content. I choose to be grateful. I choose to live in this moment. Remembering the past and having aspirations for the future, but not letting that override taking advantage of this second, this breathe, this moment. The future will come regardless of your effort to prevent it and the past is only an unchangeable memory. If you are not content with what you have and with who you are, you will not be happy if you change your circumstances. Water your grass and make it greener. Happiness is not outside yourself. These things make me happy. But we chase things, stuff, material worldly possessions like they matter. Climb the ladder, pull the levers because that is what we are supposed to do. As a nation we have forgotten how to love. We have forgotten compassion. We are siloed and broken souls walking alone amongst the crowd and we wonder- where did our laughter go? Where did our character go? Where is our happiness? So much gloom and doom and this president and this economy and this shooting- every bit of this stems from caring more about the world's definition than our own of how we should live our lives. We don't want to accept this because if we do, we will have to wake up and take responsibility for how we feel, for our actions and behaviors, we will have to take responsibility for our own lives, and it can be somehow challenging to do so-more than the clockwork scripted sadness.

We fill our lives with baubles and trinkets that don't matter, to impress people we don't know and wonder why we still feel empty inside- like our calling has no one picking up.
Be the person who gives a damn, there's already way too many who don't. You have the incredible ability to make a difference in someone's life. Answer the siren's call of the causes and people that mean the most to you. Galvanize your words with action. You have the potential to change the entire world.

ROB'S ADVICE ON DATING

"When you are a child don't throw mud at girls from the neighborhood for invading your fort, because one of them might grow up to be incredibly beautiful and won't have forgiven you for doing that when you see her again as a grown up. "

A genuine smile is the most beautiful thing a woman can wear.

87. START A COLLECTION

Decide on something that is interesting to both of you- stamps and coins are common, but has become so commercial that sometimes the true fun of discovery is lost.

This is your and his collection so keep it fun. I remember when I was a kid one of my friend's dad had the coolest action figures that you could ever imagine...all in boxes- okay yeah probably worth a mint now, but for a kid- what a ridiculous idea to get something you can't play with or hold. When your child gets older they can decide to keep a collection like that for monetary sake, but this is about having fun together. This is about creating a bond over something that has a very specific meaning to both of you and keeping on the search for it to be able to tell the other person about it. Depending on what you decide to collect, maybe you might even have some history or science you can throw in and make it a learning experience.

88. JEEPERS CREEPERS- WHERE DID YOU GET THOSE PEEPERS?

Buy your child an inexpensive microscope, a pair of binoculars or a telescope. Let them discover the magnificence of the world.

"What if today's the day you learn ostriches? You don't want to miss that, do you?" - me convincing Noah this morning to wake up when he didn't want to go to school.

89. WHAT WORK EXPERIENCE DO YOU HAVE OTHER THAN THE LEMONADE STAND?

In many important times in a person's life they are interviewed. For certain colleges, awards, grants, jobs and other things the ability to be calm and answer direct questions is a valuable skill. Although our children have the rest of their lives to be adults and we don't want them to grow up too fast, we should also understand that we are building a foundation for the long-term. Explain what an interview is and have them do one occasionally- as the applicant or as the interviewer. Get the newness (and therefor some of the nervousness) out of them by interviewing them every so often.

ROBS THOUGHT ON VOCABULARY WORDS-

When I was a child I thought it was called coward because people would run towards a cow if something was scary and hide behind them. Part of me still wonders why the word doesn't mean "toward a cow"

90. ANIMAL FARM – (THE PLACE NOT THE BOOK)

Okay, well any farm will do. Find a farm close to you that allows visitors or has tours and set it up. It's a shame that many children now grow up without having pulled a carrot from the ground or collected eggs from a henhouse. Sometimes kids don't make the correlation between farmers and what ends up on our plate, however once they visit the farm your child will realize how much work goes into working the land.

ROB'S TANGENT TIME

War

I have had the opportunity to walk among people that were willing to die for what they believed in, and in more cases that I can count- they did. We go about our lives and move forward, out of self-preservation and partly because that's what our friends that died would have wanted and mostly just because that is what is natural. I don't believe in closure-I feel that pain and hurt reminds us how much we cared for someone. Wounds don't heal, we just get used to them and the NEWNESS of the pain is the only thing that time actually affects. We shouldn't wallow in sadness or in loss, but we also can't embrace the full depth of human emotion without accepting the painful parts as well. No mountains without valleys... Some people will give you admonishments about "well they are in heaven"... I am not saddened by where they are, I am saddened by where they are not. They are not at bbq's with me while our kids run and frolic in the yard. They are not calling me in the middle of the night just to share a laugh. My friends that we lost along the way, the ones that laughed with us, cried with us, knew us better than most- there is not a day that goes by that I don't think to myself- Would you be proud of me, was my life worth it? So I try to be a great father, make the world a better place and be a great friend- someone whose life is worth it. However the sacrifice wasn't for Robert Urban. They didn't die for just me - they died for all of us. Although they didn't know you or perhaps wouldn't even like you they still died for you. So that means your life has value, someone sacrificed growing old and their potential so you could have yours. You don't need to start a charity or fly flags or shout ooh-rah! at parades, but do the things that make anyone's sacrifice worth it. Live your life to its fullest measure, be better than you were yesterday, raise good kids that value respect and hard work, augh with friends, forgive others and yourself for mistakes, kiss your spouse and tell him or her why you love them and why, make time for those who love you. Take the time today- five minutes- to write or text a friend or family member thanking them or just telling them you love them, for no other reason than simply you do.

91. CREATE A SUPER HERO.

Anyone can be a super hero and this is fun because it encourages your child to be their own super hero. While we have the batman versus superman debate often at the house and I am now a marvel and DC expert, it is so much better when the child is the one saving the day.

Have them create a list of ways they could be a super hero and what they would do, Learning that a hero's everyday actions are more empowering than being a star is awesome. We have to create the need for children to look up to who they are, Others will always let you down, it's human, it can't be helped., But when you do something that disappoints yourself,- you learn that you have the power to change it! You can't change other super hero's! Have them get creative They could even draw a cartoon of them in action. Design a certain logo, make a chart for their room where they can monitor their super heroness! This teaches control of ones actions, and empowers them to make a difference and to understand the simple things are indeed heroic.

"Your shoes are on the wrong feet"
"I don't have any other feet than these"

92. STICKS AND STONES WILL BREAK YOUR BONES...AND WORDS CAN HURT YOU

Sticks and stones may break my bones, but names will never hurt me." – that's a lie we must stop telling our kids. People can tell a girl she is beautiful a million times and she may not believe it, but someone calls her ugly once and she believes it the rest of her life. I know a woman who is dear to me who doesn't think she is beautiful; when in reality she is the definition of beauty because her heart is diamonds and her mind is wildfire.

So we have to be careful what we say and what we teach our children, because words are so powerful. Yet on the other hand, (and this might sound insensitive), but has bullying really gotten that bad or as a society are we too sensitive about people (especially children) getting their feelings hurt? And, I don't mean this toward students who are ostracized for issues like sexual orientation, race, religion, financial status, etc. and think any physical aggression is definitely crossing the line. I know emotional damage is worse than physical and kids can be so cruel...but sometimes life is hard and mean as well Are we doing our children a disservice by running to their aid **EVERY** time someone says their ears are too big? Bullying has changed faces thanks to the internet and the feeling anonymity gives many people the freedom to say whatever the hell they want and they often do.

93. THE LIFE AND TIMES OF A CHILD- AN AUTOBIOGRAPHY

Have your child write their autobiography, Use small spiral notebooks for this. Create a cover with cardboard or hard paper and then fill with notebook paper and punch holes and pull yarn or ribbon down the side. You will want them to date this and make one once a year. It will be interesting for your child to tune into their life and the people in it. Their accomplishments and their likes and dislikes. It will show their changes in themselves and their growth. It will also be a fun thing to read later for them to remember if there was something they really wanted to do, but things might have got in the way! It's never too late to learn about you!

94. DO THE RIGHT THING BECAUSE IT'S THE RIGHT THING

Noah and I were running some errands earlier today and he saw a man in a wheelchair leaving the bank.
Noah ran across the bank to the door and opened it for him and the old man snapped at him that "I can open my own damn door".
Noah came back very upset and told me what happened. I hustled Noah out to catch up to the old man.
He had not gone far, when I walked up to him and said "I understand pride and being a man, but this is a young child who was trying to be courteous and kind to you and being disabled doesn't give you the right to talk to him and treat him like you did.

The old man looked at me and then to Noah and extended his hand which Noah shook.
"I am sorry I talked to you like that young man. Your dad is right."
He nodded at me and we went back to the day.

I talked to Noah on the drive to our next place about pride and why the old man didn't want help, but that we open doors for women, old people and the disabled not because of who they are, but because of who we are.

95. ETHNIC ABSORPTION.

Plan a meal where you indulge in a specific ethnic evening. Have your children help plan the meal, and pick the challenge. An example would be Hopi Indian Bread as a treat for Indian night. Dress the part, get out the drums and shakers, put on music for dinner like "Dream Catcher, Tokeya Inajin (Kevin Locke) this is beautiful flute music! Do an African Tribal music with collard greens. Have an Italian night! This will be great for teaching children about other cultures and appreciation of different foods and music. Find music on line to assist you and gather some awesome recipes. Have children help in sticking to a budget, but indulging in the moment of learning and fun. Don't forget the Australian Aboriginal didgeridoo music and dinner.

The reason we struggle with insecurity is because **we compare our behind-the-scenes** with everyone else's highlight reel.- Steve Furtick

ROB'S LETTER TO DEADBEAT DADS

Hey deadbeats. Quit being a piece of crap and take care of your responsibilities. Apologize to your kids and spend the next few years making up for it. We all make mistakes, but here is the trick- be there. Be an example. Not just an example- a good example. You don't need to be rich or smart or creative to be an awesome parent, just give a damn about your kids and spend time with them. The world is an amazing place, and it's your job to engage your children in the task of learning about it. Your children are your responsibility, your gift, your letter to the world in the future. I have friends that are deployed and would give anything to see their kids and play with them. I drop off my son to his mom's house on her days and my heart breaks. If you had a bad childhood, who cares. You are not your past. Grow a set and be a man and teach your kids about character and life and be someone who they should want to be like. Real men love their kids.

ROB THE MOVIE CRITIC

Scarface didn't really give those guys enough time to say "hello" before shooting them.

ROB THE BOOK CRITIC

How many of you remember the story "The Giving Tree?" I have always thought that little boy took advantage of the tree's kindness and he was a horrible kid. I also never liked the Rudolph the red-nosed reindeer because no one appreciated him until they benefitted from him and no one apologized.

ROB'S TANGENT TIME

My Teribithia

"You can never go back again." When I was a child, I had a secret place. You took the path to Eagle creek, cut through Brantons pond and about 50 feet further there was a hidden path to an old abandoned treehouse in the woods. You could still see the pond and had the shade and comfort of your fort. That was my

Teribithia... When I just needed to be alone with my thoughts or simply just have my own fortress of solitude, I would hop on my bike and this is where I would often go. But time passes and we grow older and things like girls, career choices and school matter more. And that fort soon became abandoned again. When I was last in Summerville, South Carolina a few months back, I took Noah exploring and took him there to see if the old fort still stood. It did, but the reality of it was far less great than my memory of it. Where I had remembered it being a hundred feet in the air, it was more like ten. And what I had considered as a marvel of engineering was lucky to have ever bore weight at all. We often look at events and people in our past and long for the "good old days". I am not sure if it is a safety mechanism, but we often remember things far better than what they were. Pain often dulls, but the good memories shine brighter with age. Often we wonder why we ever broke up with someone or we wish we could visit a place again with the new and wonderful perspective and maturity. The truth is that often the best place for things of the past are in the past. I am 35 here in a November and would say there are three distinct chapters in my life. My birth until I graduated, my time in the Marines and since then. Every chapter I am someone different- building on and appreciating my past and having the same character traits, but different from how the world views me. At 25, I thought I knew everything. I had been around the world and had experiences that most people could only dream of. 34 year old Robert thinks 25 year old Rob was an idiot. I often wonder if 45 year old Rob is going to think the same of today's Rob or if we do hit our top level in our 30's? I am the sum of my experiences from all of these chapters in my life. To steal from Chuck Palahniuk "I am the combined effort of everyone I ever met." We all are. I tell myself that when I meet someone new, they too have different chapters and experiences that led them to today. Someone sent me a private message a few month's back stating that they didn't think I would turn out to be a good father. Her last knowledge of me was when I was 16. I don't think anyone sees a 16 year old and thinks, he is going to be a good dad. That is before we became a man. I think people see us in the prism of how they met or in what capacity they know us from, often not the complete who we are. We are made up of the texture of their experience at a certain moment in their life, but the reality of us is much more complex and beautiful. All this diatribe is to remind you that sometimes, the past is best left in the past and to embrace the friendships, the experiences and the laughter of this moment. Carpe Diem.

96. ENCOURAGE YOUR CHILD IN ALL THINGS

Noah swims, plays soccer, competes in martial arts and other sports. He has some natural talent, an athletic build and a fierce work ethic. Regardless of the sport or venue I tell him the same thing before any meet/game/fight or even practice. "Have fun and give it your best effort." One morning Noah had an early game and one of the kids on the opposing team wasn't as good of an athlete as some of the other kids on the field. His father was screaming admonishments the entire game, things like "Why did you let him pass you? "Don't let that kid make you look stupid again." After that remark I went up to him and tactfully just tried to strike conversation in order to defuse the bomb a little. My heart was broken for his kid. He asked which one was mine and I pointed him out. "Your kid is awesome, I wish mine was like that." I responded "I hope our children never point to someone else and say "That parent is awesome, I wish mine was like that." Not sure if he got the gist of what I meant or if he was too absorbed, but he didn't respond and the game ended shortly thereafter. After I dropped Noah off it got me thinking not just about kids, but what message do we have for anyone in every stage of life. "Have fun and give it your best effort"-seems like advice that we should take for every endeavor. Fun doesn't necessarily mean the bells and whistles of the midway, but perhaps a sense of accomplishment in a job well done or pride in an honest day's work. The knowledge that in some small way the world or someone's life is better directly because of your effort. In everything, give your all.

97. A BETTER MOUSETRAP

Outside of their natural tendency to love, a child's imagination is their second greatest asset. Harness that by solving a problem- inventing something that would make the world a better place. You start the brainstorm by asking questions such as; wouldn't it be cool if? Or identifying a common problem that needs to be solved. (In this day and age this is also how mobile apps are developed. The technology is the easy part, the what is it solving is the key.) Once you have some ideas, have your child try to implement them with looking things up, drawings and talking about it taking notes! Not only is this awesome, but it teaches your child so long as they keep thinking they can make a difference in the world. Their invention may or may not work, but it teaches discipline, focus, and self importance.

Noah came up with a really good idea and we joked that spies were going to steal it so we wrote down the idea with lemon juice and a q-tip so that would disappear until reactivated by heat.

TANGENT TIME

Quarter Life Update

I'm not a big believer in regrets. I believe for the most part that we made the best of what knowledge we had at the time and for the most part when we made whatever choice it was, it was exactly what we wanted at that moment. The things I regret are not the things I did or poor choices I might have made, but rather the things I didn't do. The girl I didn't talk to, the person I didn't help when I could have, the time's I didn't stop to smell the proverbial roses. As far as my mistakes, and I have made many, I like to think that I have often learned a valuable truth or a lesson from them... and overall my life is pretty great and mistakes were part of my path getting here. If I had some magic wand, would I change things? I'm not so sure... I might not have gotten married, so that I would never have gotten divorced...(a small part of me still gets jealous when I see a happy couple with a kid- that was supposed to be my life) but then I wouldn't have Noah, nor the relationship I enjoy. I wouldn't live in Orlando and have the great friends I love dearly here. I am happy. I look forward to the possibilities of tomorrow. I am motivated about believing I can still change myself and the world for the better. If we are honest with ourselves, what makes us happy? What do we want out of life? Are you able to observe yourself from time to time and see whether the things you chase after are really the things you want for yourself or are they things society dangles in front of you? I think that most of us, want more than we have, because when we live in such a disposable world we go on the next thing so easily. Things easily lose that sparkle so we go on, then on to the next thing, and the next thing, and this is how most of us spend our lives, running after something that we think it is outside ourselves, believing that our happiness lies in things, in other people, in different places, etc., and we rarely or never, stop to observe ourselves and our behavior. We rarely or never stop to think whether we are sane or insane for doing so. Know yourself. Challenge yourself to do the things that scare you, because these are the only way we grow. Find and embrace the child that still lives within you- not impressed by bank accounts or the car someone drives or the house they own, but rather on their character or if they are funny or kind. It is never too late to return to yourself. I challenge you to start observing your thoughts, analyze the why of your goals and live deliberately. Discover who you are and walk down the path that makes your heart soar. And doing so will inspire others to do the same, and this is how we change the world. So here is to a pretty good first half of my life. You are incredible, powerful beyond measure and deserve for your dreams to come true.

98. THE FEAR JAR

Both you and your child write a list of 5 or 10 things you're afraid of (even spiders). Then write down ways to overcome the fear. Decide if it's an illogical fear versus a real fear. First, you may learn some things about your child and be able to use this time to reinforce they are safe or best practices in case it is a real fear (like teaching what to do if bitten by a snake if one of the written fears is a snake.) Take all of the written fears and put them in a sealable jar and seal it together. This teaches them to confront blocks in their way and helps them understand that if there are some fears you can't change, there are ways to deal with them.

INFIDELITY

Infidelity is never the person who was cheated on's fault. It is never because you weren't pretty enough or didn't pay attention to his needs or any other such pansy ass excuse. Infidelity is a character flaw, plain and simple. Before you decide to go prancing about to see what the grass on the other side is like either have the honor, respect and the stones to break it off with your partner before you do or hey even better water your own damn grass and rediscover the spark that attracted you to each other in the first place.

99. FAV THIS

You can tell what someone values by what they treasure. During any meal ask them what their favorite book is. Ask them why?

Have them describe what happens in the story. You can do this with movies or computer games or a favorite day they had during the week- anything favorite. This teaches them to recall things and to communicate that to someone else with descriptive language and clarity. More importantly you can get a glimpse of their priorities. Kids can also tell what you value by what you compliment. Instead of telling your daughter she is beautiful, tell her she is smart or another characteristic that matters.

TANGENT TIME

I Wish I Could Protect Them All

"I wish somehow I could protect you all" My heart breaks for the abused child. For the child betrayed by the person who is supposed to protect him. When Noah was a child and had any fear he would run into my arms and know that I could and would protect him against anything. When he got to the age of monsters in the closet I told him to pretend that we were asleep and to let me know when he saw them. When he did I tackled a pile of clothes in his closet while he laughed. I walked back over to his bed and gave him a boxing glove and said it was magic and that monsters were afraid of it and if the monsters ever scared him just put on the boxing glove and they wouldn't mess with him. On more than one occasion I would check on him in the middle of the night to find him sleeping peacefully with the glove on his hand and laughing in his sleep. These are the easy monsters. The tough monsters are the one that are supposed to love us. The monsters with anger cached-easily becoming volcanoes at the slightest wrong- hatred and pain of their past crashing through the levy and breaking through their soul to justify hitting a child. The monster excuses such behavior with clever hollow idioms such as "a lesson needs to be taught" The only lesson that is taught is how to slowly die inside until one day there is a very good chance that your child will become a monster too.

But sometimes they don't become monsters. Sometimes they just become broken. People who feel like because they were once broken that they could never be beautiful or because they weren't loved that they didn't and don't deserve to be. For those who are grown and lived past the monsters- a quiet hushed secret becomes laid in closets next to your other skeletons. If you think for one second no one knows where you have been, be accepting of the fact that you are wrong, that the long drought of despair and blame that you drank from has been drank by many - that pain is part of this thing called the human condition and you were never alone. I wish somehow I could protect you all. Not everyone has the strength needed to stand there, wait for it to end and believe every things gonna be OK. But if you choose to break the cycle, you choose to rise victorious- a phoenix that says it ended with me and tomorrow will be different, then it will be more than okay. It will be your greatest moment, a monumental triumph. If you have rage or someone destroyed your childhood or you walk with a demon that only you know, get it off your chest. Forgive them, not for their sake, but for yours. Not because they deserve forgiveness, but because you deserve to let go.

100. X-RAY VISION

Teach them to see what is inside. Once when my son was very young we were in a Barnes and Noble and a handicapped child made a low wailing sound. To my embarrassment, Noah mimicked the sound as loud as he could. I shuttled him out of there as fast as I could with many parents looking at me like I was the worst person in the world. When we got outside, I asked Noah why he did that. He told me that the kid was being silly so he was being silly back. He didn't see the kid as any different- just thought he was being a kid. I was the one who needed a lesson that day...I spoke to Noah about disabilities and people being different than one another, but didn't feel like I got the point until I thought of this. We went to Wal-Mart and bought paper cups. We colored some, painted some, and glued some stuff on, cut parts out, almost anything crafty you can imagine. Once everything was dry I put all of the cups over different numbers of pieces of chocolate. I then asked Noah to tell me which ones had something great in it. I showed him that they all did, but there was no way of knowing until we looked inside. Use this activity to teach compassion and that we shouldn't judge anyone based on their outward appearance.

There are wish bones, jaw bones, and back bones. Those who dream about doing things, those who talk about doing things, and those who actually accomplish things. Always try to be the back bone.

101. LOVE SIGNS

Noah is a swimmer. At meets he typically can't distinguish one voice from the other so many years ago I taught him the I love you sign language. When dropping him off at school or his mom's, he looks back and we make the sign to each other. Make a sign or gesture (or use this one) to be able to non-verbally tell your child you love them and are able to communicate that over long distances, or the den of noise.

This is the secret to raising a child to be great: Be a great example yourself. Your child will follow your example, not solely your advice.

Made in the USA
San Bernardino, CA
22 March 2016